W9-ALL-566

DATE DUE

GAYLORD			PRINTED IN U.S.A.

FAIR HAVEN LIBRARY
182 GRAND AVENUE
NEW HAVEN, CT 06513

IDA B. WELLS-BARNETT

Other titles in the *African-American Biography Library*

BOOKER T. WASHINGTON
"Character Is Power"
ISBN-13: 978-0-7660-2535-6
ISBN-10:   0-7660-2535-7

COLIN POWELL
"Have a Vision. Be Demanding"
ISBN-13: 978-0-7660-2464-9
ISBN-10:   0-7660-2464-4

DUKE ELLINGTON
"I Live With Music"
ISBN-13: 978-0-7660-2702-2
ISBN-10:   0-7660-2702-3

GWENDOLYN BROOKS
"Poetry Is Life Distilled"
ISBN-13: 978-0-7660-2292-8
ISBN-10:   0-7660-2292-7

JACKIE ROBINSON
"All I Ask Is That You Respect
Me as a Human Being"
ISBN-13: 978-0-7660-2461-8
ISBN-10:   0-7660-2461-X

LANGSTON HUGHES
"Life Makes Poems"
ISBN-13: 978-0-7660-2468-7
ISBN-10:   0-7660-2468-7

LOUIS ARMSTRONG
"Jazz Is Played From
The Heart"
ISBN-13: 978-0-7660-2700-8
ISBN-10:   0-7660-2700-7

MARTIN LUTHER KING, JR.
"We Shall Overcome"
ISBN-13: 978-0-7660-1774-0
ISBN-10:   0-7660-1774-5

MAYA ANGELOU
"Diversity Makes For
a Rich Tapestry"
ISBN-13: 978-0-7660-2469-4
ISBN-10:   0-7660-2469-5

MUHAMMAD ALI
"I Am the Greatest"
ISBN-13: 978-0-7660-2460-1
ISBN-10:   0-7660-2460-1

OPRAH WINFREY
"I Don't Believe in Failure"
ISBN-13: 978-0-7660-2462-5
ISBN-10:   0-7660-2462-8

PAUL ROBESON
"I Want to Make Freedom Ring"
ISBN-13: 978-0-7660-2703-9
ISBN-10:   0-7660-2703-1

RAY CHARLES
"I Got Music Inside Me"
ISBN-13: 978-0-7660-2701-5
ISBN-10:   0-7660-2701-5

ROSA PARKS
"Tired of Giving In"
ISBN-13:   978-0-7660-2463-2
ISBN-10: 0-7660-2463-6

WILL SMITH
"I Like Blending a Message
With Comedy"
ISBN-13: 978-0-7660-2465-6
ISBN-10:   0-7660-2465-2

ZORA NEALE HURSTON
"I Have Been In
Sorrow's Kitchen"
ISBN-13: 978-0-7660-2536-3
ISBN-10:   0-7660-2536-5

IDA B. WELLS-BARNETT

"Strike a Blow Against a Glaring Evil"

Anne Schraff

Series Consultant:
Dr. Russell L. Adams, Chairman
Department of
Afro-American Studies,
Howard University

Enslow Publishers, Inc.
40 Industrial Road
Box 398
Berkeley Heights, NJ 07922
USA
http://www.enslow.com

"THEY SIMPLY COULDN'T UNDERSTAND WHY ONE WOULD RISK A GOOD JOB, EVEN FOR THEIR CHILDREN. . . . BUT I THOUGHT IT WAS RIGHT TO STRIKE A BLOW AGAINST A GLARING EVIL. . . ."

—Ida B. Wells-Barnett on why she risked her teaching job, which she soon lost, to write a newspaper essay criticizing the poor conditions of the public schools in Memphis, Tennessee.

Copyright © 2008 by Anne Schraff

All rights reserved.

No part of this book may be reproduced by any means without the written permission of the publisher.

Library of Congress Cataloging-in-Publication Data

Schraff, Anne E.
      Ida B. Wells-Barnett : "strike a blow against a glaring evil" / by Anne Schraff.
         p. cm. — (African-American biography library)
      Summary: "Discusses Ida B. Wells-Barnett's life, her work as a teacher, writer, civil rights activist, and her strong stand against lynching in the late 19th and early 20th centuries"— Provided by publisher.
      Includes bibliographical references and index.
      ISBN-13: 978-0-7660-2704-6
      ISBN-10: 0-7660-2704-X
      1. Wells-Barnett, Ida B., 1862–1931—Juvenile literature. 2. African American women civil rights workers—Biography—Juvenile literature. 3. Civil rights workers—United States— Biography—Juvenile literature. 4. African American women journalists—Biography—Juvenile literature. 5. African American women educators—Biography—Juvenile literature. 6. African Americans—Biography—Juvenile literature. 7. Lynching—United States—History—Juvenile literature. 8. United States—Race relations—Juvenile literature. I. Title.
      E185.97.W55S37 2008
      323.092—dc22
      [B]
                                        2007016051

Printed in the United States of America

10 9 8 7 6 5 4 3 2 1

Illustration Credits: Courtesy of the Allen-Littlefield Collection, 56; Arkansas History Commission, pp. 5, 7 (center), 11 (center), 19 (center), 27 (center), 38 (center), 50 (center), 62 (center), 76 (center), 87 (center), 99 (center), 106; Associated Press, 110; © 2001 Chesapeake & Ohio Historical Society, p. 9; Chicago Historical Society, p. 105; Department of Special Collections, the University of Chicago Library, pp. 6, 7 (left and right), 11 (left and right), 19 (left and right), 27 (left and right), 38 (left and right), 50 (left and right), 62 (left and right), 76 (left and right), 87 (left and right), 99 (left and right), 43, 71, 82, 90; Used with permission of Documenting the American South, The University of North Carolina at Chapel Hill Libraries, pp. 33, 40; Enslow Publishers, Inc., p. 12; The Granger Collection, New York, p. 58; Courtesy of The Ida B. Wells Memorial Foundation, p. 15; Library of Congress, pp. 18, 21, 28, 64, 83, 88, 97, 108; Marshall County Historical Museum, Holly Springs, Mississippi, pp. 13, 25; Ohio Historical Center Archives, p. 74; Schomburg Center for Research in Black Culture, The New York Public Library, pp. 36, 66, 78.

Cover Illustration: Department of Special Collections, the University of Chicago Library.

Contents

Ida B. Wells-Barnett

Chapter 1

The First Battle

On May 4, 1884, twenty-two-year-old Ida Wells, an African-American teacher, boarded the Chesapeake and Ohio Railroad. She was going from her home in Memphis to her teaching job in Woodstock, Tennessee. Wells had bought a first-class ticket, which entitled her to a seat in the ladies' coach. When the conductor came to collect the tickets, he refused to accept hers. He told Wells to move to the smoker's car, where black men and women were seated. Wells refused to leave the seat for which she had paid.[1] Ida Wells had been reading a book, and she continued reading, ignoring the conductor's demands. The conductor removed her baggage and her umbrella, telling Wells again to get out of her seat and move to the second-class car designated for black passengers.[2]

Segregation in the South

In the years just after the Civil War, African Americans in the South enjoyed the rights of all Americans. They voted, and many African Americans were elected to high office in state and federal governments. Pinckney Stewart Pinchback became lieutenant governor of Louisiana. Johnathan Wright became associate justice in the State Supreme Court of South Carolina. Hiram Revels and Blanche K. Bruce became U.S. senators from Mississippi.

By the late 1870s, this began to change. The white people in the South imposed a system of segregation, which slowly deprived African Americans of the right to vote and other basic human rights. By law and custom, African Americans were forced to accept separate and inferior facilities in schools, transportation, jobs, and housing. The federal government did nothing to change the fact that African Americans were now second-class citizens.

When Ida Wells continued to refuse to leave her seat, the conductor grabbed her arm and began pulling her up. Wells held onto the back of the seat in front of her and firmly braced her feet. Wells later described what she did when the conductor yanked harder on her arm: "I fastened my teeth in the back of his hand."[3]

The bleeding conductor was then helped by other passengers. He and the others dragged Wells from her seat and down the aisle. Wells described how the white passengers "stood on their seats so that they could get a good view and continued applauding the conductor for his brave stand."[4] When Wells realized they were going to force her to sit in the smoking car, she agreed to leave the train. At the next stop, her hair disheveled and the sleeve of her blouse torn, Wells stepped onto the station platform.

Above is the Louisa, Kentucky depot of the Chattaroi Railroad in 1880, which later became the Chesapeake & Ohio Railroad.

Ida Wells sued the railroad for the incident. Memphis Circuit Court Judge James A. Pierce ruled that the civil rights of Ida Wells had been violated when she was forced from the seat for which she had paid. She was awarded five hundred dollars in damages, but the railroad appealed the case. In 1887, the Tennessee State Supreme Court reversed the decision, and Wells had to pay court costs. "I felt so disappointed," Wells later wrote in her diary. "I had hoped [for] such great things from the suit for my people generally."[5]

Chapter 2

Mississippi Childhood

Ida Bell Wells was born on July 16, 1862, in the northern Mississippi town of Holly Springs. It was a small cotton plantation town in the 1830s, but by the 1850s it had an iron foundry. The main office of the Mississippi Central Railroad was located there. Although little fighting took place in Holly Springs when the Civil War began in 1861, rival armies took the town several times during the war. It was a Union army depot when Ida was five months old. Confederate forces took control, burning and damaging the business district of Holly Springs, along with many beautiful homes.

Ida's mother, Elizabeth Warrenton, known as Lizzie, was one of ten children born to slave parents in Virginia. When Elizabeth was seven years old, she and two of her sisters were taken from their parents and sold into slavery in Mississippi. Elizabeth was sold to several different

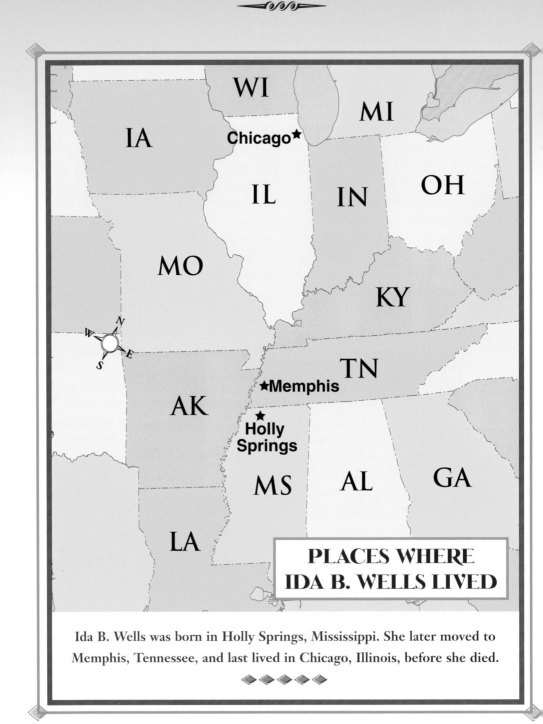

PLACES WHERE IDA B. WELLS LIVED

Ida B. Wells was born in Holly Springs, Mississippi. She later moved to Memphis, Tennessee, and last lived in Chicago, Illinois, before she died.

Above is a picture of an African-American family who lived
in Holly Springs, Mississippi, around the time that Ida was born.

owners, and she suffered from abuse. Finally she was sold
to Spires Bolling, a wealthy white building contractor in
Holly Springs. She was trained to be a cook for the Bolling
household.

Ida's father, James Wells, had a less harsh life as a slave.
He was born on a plantation in Tippah County,
Mississippi, the son of his white master and a black slave
named Peggy. James Wells's father had no children by his
wife, Polly, and he loved his slave son. Polly Wells resented

her husband's relationship with Peggy. When James was eighteen, his father took him to Spires Bolling and asked Bolling to train the boy as an apprentice carpenter. When James Wells's father died, his wife was able to take revenge on Peggy, whom she had "stripped and whipped."[1] Many years later, when his mother told him that Polly Wells wished to see him, James Wells said, "I never want to see that old woman as long as I live."[2] He could not forget what she had done to his mother.

While they both worked at the Bolling plantation, James Wells and Elizabeth Warrenton fell in love and began living together. They could not marry legally, because they were slaves. When the Civil War ended in 1865 and they were emancipated, or freed, James and Elizabeth were officially married. Ida was three years old at the time. Seven more children were born to the union, four boys and three girls.

James and Elizabeth Wells were still living in the house Bolling had provided them when the Civil War ended. James Wells continued working for Bolling, but now Wells was receiving wages as a free man. With so much destruction from the war, there was plenty of work for a carpenter. Wells helped rebuild the homes and businesses that had been damaged during the past four years.[3]

Elizabeth Wells was a deeply religious woman, and one of her strongest goals was to find her parents and her brothers and sisters. She had not heard anything from them since she was a young child. Separation from family, often forever, was one of the cruelest aspects of the slave system. As adults, many slaves yearned to see the beloved faces of lost mothers and fathers, brothers, and sisters.

James Wells was a hardworking, skilled carpenter who saved as much of his wages as he could. His interest in politics led to trouble with his employer. Spires Bolling, like almost all white Southerners, was a Democrat. He told all of his employees to vote Democrat. James Wells and

Ida B. Wells was born on the grounds of the
Spires Bolling House in Holly Springs, Mississippi.
Today, the house is the site of the Ida B. Wells-Barnett Museum.

the other freedmen had not been able to vote as slaves, but they now had the right to vote. Since Republican Abraham Lincoln had freed the slaves, most black men, including Wells, were Republicans. When Bolling learned that Wells had voted Republican, Bolling ordered Wells from the house he was using and fired him from his job. Wells used his savings to buy a house for his family, as well as his own set of tools, and he went into business for himself. He made much more money this way.

Though James Wells probably never learned to read well, he believed strongly in education. He was eager for his children to go to school. Rust College (first known as Shaw University) was founded in Holly Springs in 1866 by the Freedman's Aid Society of the Episcopal Church. The founders were missionaries from the North, and the school provided basic elementary education for African-American children and adults. James Wells was elected to the first board of trustees at the school.[4] Education was a major

Rust College Today

Rust College is the second oldest private college in Mississippi. It is an accredited four-year liberal arts college with more than a thousand students. Most are African American, but other races are welcome.

The spacious campus now hosts many community and cultural events. The library is named for a famous African-American, Mississippi-born opera singer Leontyne Price.

value to both of Ida Wells's parents. "Our job was to go to school," Ida Wells later recalled.[5]

When Ida started school, her mother accompanied her. This was common at Rust College, as no education at all had been provided for African Americans during slavery. Elizabeth Wells wanted to learn to read so she could read the Bible. She wanted to write letters to people in Virginia who might help her find her lost family. She did learn to read; but in spite of all her efforts, she never found out what happened to her family.

After school at night, Ida read the newspaper to her father and his friends who gathered around the kitchen table. At this time, the number of African-American politicians was rising in Mississippi. State Senator Hiram Revels was about to go to Washington as a U.S. senator from Mississippi. The idea of African-American men being sworn in as senators in Washington, D.C., was encouraging to James Wells and the other men who were working for a bright future for their children.

As the oldest of eight children, Ida had many chores around her house. It was her job to give the younger children their Saturday night baths. She laid out their clothing and polished their shoes in preparation for Sunday church services. The Wells family belonged to the Asbury Methodist Church. They attended services so faithfully that Elizabeth Wells won a prize for perfect attendance.

HEROES OF THE COLORED RACE.

Senator Hiram Revels (right) can be seen in this poster, along with black former abolitionist and author Frederick Douglass (center) and Senator Blanche Bruce.

After church, the family read the Bible at home and visited neighboring relatives. Ida was baptized at age twelve.

Ida continued her education at Rust College, which was now offering a high school program that prepared students for a teaching career. Ida was a very good student, and she enjoyed studying. However, in 1878, a terrible tragedy was to strike Holly Springs, an event that would change Ida Wells's future forever.

Chapter 3

Head of the Family and Teacher

Yellow fever is a severe viral disease that killed many people in the eighteenth and nineteenth centuries. It causes bleeding from the eyes and nostrils and attacks the liver, the kidneys, and the heart. When it strikes the liver, the patient's skin turns yellow, giving the disease its name. For a long time, nobody knew how the disease spread. They feared it was passed from person to person. Then in 1898, Dr. Walter Reed discovered the disease was spread by the bite of a mosquito.

In 1878, a mild winter in the South was followed by an early spring and then a hot summer. These were ideal conditions for the breeding of mosquitoes. Yellow fever swept through the Mississippi Valley from New Orleans to

Tennessee. It struck most heavily in low-lying areas where there were many swamps. Holly Springs was built at a higher elevation and had never suffered an outbreak of the disease. This year was different.

Ida Wells was on a visit to her grandmother Peggy's farm in Marshall County, about thirty miles from Holly Springs, in September of 1878. When she left home, everyone in her family was well. When yellow fever broke out in Holly Springs, Ida was not aware of it, isolated as she was on her grandmother's farm.

Yellow fever had broken out in Memphis, Tennessee,

The Dreaded Fever

Yellow fever was one of the most dreaded diseases in the United States in the 1700s and 1800s. When it struck Philadelphia in 1793, hundreds fled the city. They were turned away from New York at gunpoint.[1] The official death toll in Philadelphia was almost four thousand people. In 1797, Philadelphia was again stricken, and this time eleven hundred died.

By the end of the century, yellow fever had claimed an estimated ten thousand lives in the United States and many more in Italy, France, Spain, and England. The 1878 outbreak in the Mississippi Valley that devastated Holly Springs was one of the last serious outbreaks in the United States.[2]

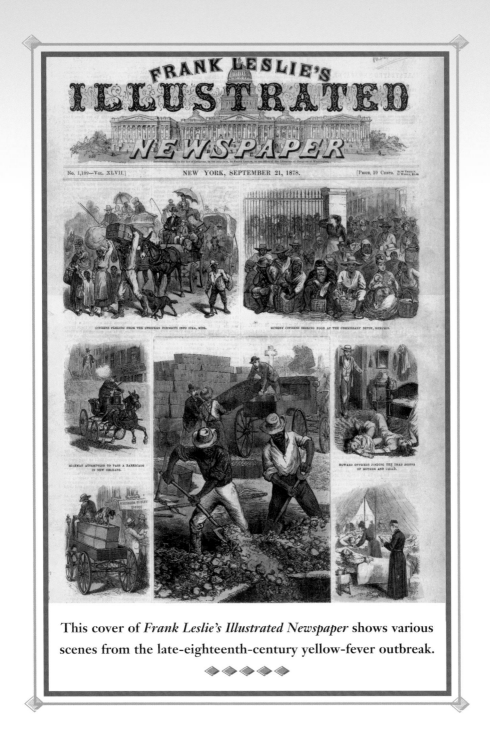

This cover of *Frank Leslie's Illustrated Newspaper* shows various scenes from the late-eighteenth-century yellow-fever outbreak.

fifty miles from Holly Springs. People fled Memphis and came to Holly Springs. When cases began to appear in Holly Springs, many residents fled in terror in wagons, buggies, or on horseback. Some even walked out of town. Stores were closed, and trading ceased. Holly Springs became a ghost town when white and black people began dying of the disease.

One day, three men from Holly Springs came riding up to Ida's grandmother's farm. They had been told that Ida Wells was visiting there. They had a letter for her. They hailed Ida and handed her the letter. The sixteen-year-old girl read the message. . . . "Jim and Lizzie Wells have both died of the fever, within twenty-four hours of each other. The children are all at home."[3]

Upon reading the terrible news, Ida fainted. When she recovered, she was told that the people from the Howard Association (similar to today's Red Cross) were caring for her orphaned brothers and sisters until their family could be contacted. Ida decided to go home at once. Ida's grand-mother and others urged her to wait until doctors could assure her it was safe to go to Holly Springs, but Ida ignored the warnings and packed her bag to go home. "I am the oldest of seven living children," she later recalled saying. "There's nobody but me to look after them now."[4] (Eight children were born to the family, but a few years earlier another son, Eddie, had died of spinal meningitis, a brain virus.)

Ida traveled home by train. When she arrived home, she found that all the children had been stricken, but only the youngest, baby Stanley, was still sick. On October 3, nine-month-old Stanley died of yellow fever.

Ida began caring for her brothers and sisters, which included Eugenia, fourteen; James, eleven; George, nine; Annie, five; and Lily, two.

Ida's father had been a carpenter and a mason, so he belonged to the Masonic Lodge. This group provided charitable assistance to members and their families in times of trouble. The Masons offered to help Ida take care of her family problems. On a Sunday afternoon in November 1878, members of the Masonic Lodge came to the Wellses' home with suggestions. They knew that Eugenia, the second oldest child in the family, had become disabled. Her spinal cord had begun to bend outward, and now she was bent over nearly double and could not walk. They concluded that Eugenia could not care for herself, since she was so disabled. They felt she should be sent to the poorhouse, an institution of that time that cared for the sick and the old who had no other place to go. Two of the Masons' wives offered to take Annie and Lily and raise them in their families. The men promised to get James and George enrolled in an apprentice carpentry program where their needs would be met. As for Ida, because she was sixteen, they felt she could take care of herself.

Ida Wells was horrified by the suggestion that her family would be split up. She later recalled thinking, "They were not going to put any of the children anywhere."[5] The only request Ida made of the Masons was that they help her find work so she could support her family while keeping them all together in the home. At sixteen years old, Ida had become the head of the household.

Because of the thrift and foresight of Ida's parents, they had completely paid for their home, and it was free of mortgage. There was also three hundred dollars in the bank, which Ida's parents had put away for an emergency. The teenage Ida was sure she could manage. The cash would take care of the family until she had a paycheck coming in.

The Masons arranged for Ida to be interviewed for a teaching position at a country school six miles from Holly Springs. Ida tied up her long hair and lengthened her skirt so she would look older and more suitable to be a teacher. She went to the interview and passed the teacher's examination. She was hired at a salary of twenty-five dollars a month.

Ida relied on her grandmother Peggy and some kind neighbors to help with the children while she was at work. Every Sunday afternoon, Ida rode a large white mule to her teaching job in a one-room schoolhouse. She remained there during the week, living with the parents of various students until Friday afternoon, when she would

Above is the school where Ida B. Wells taught.

ride her mule home. It was common in that time for teachers to board with the parents of their students during the week.

On the weekends, Ida washed, ironed, and cooked for her brothers and sisters. It was a hard life for a young woman. Her only recreation was reading. At the country school where she taught, there was often no oil for the lamps and no spare candles, so on dark days Ida and the children read by the light of a blazing wood fire. She read all the books she could get her hands on. She especially liked authors Charles Dickens, Louisa May Alcott, and Charlotte Brontë. She read Shakespeare as well. Later, Ida Wells lamented that among all those books, she had never read anything about people like herself. "I had never read a Negro book or anything about Negroes."[6]

Ida taught for several years in country schools, earning a reputation as a competent professional.[7] In 1883, she received an invitation from her aunt, Fannie Butler, her father's sister, to come to Memphis to live with her and her family. Aunt Belle, Ida's mother's sister, offered to take Eugenia as well as George and James, who would begin work as carpenter's apprentices. Twenty-one-year-old Ida Wells took her two younger sisters and headed for Memphis and a much different life than she had ever known.

Chapter 4

The Birth of a Journalist

When Ida B. Wells arrived in Memphis, Tennessee, in 1883, she found a bustling city with seven rail lines. It was a major cotton exchange and distribution center for grains and livestock.[1] Many freed blacks had settled in Memphis and were becoming successful. Resentment was rising among some in the white community.[2]

When Wells secured a job teaching in Woodstock, a small town ten miles outside the city, she joined an elite group of African Americans. Teachers were highly regarded, and even the white newspapers referred to them by titles of "Mr." and "Miss" and "Mrs." This kind of respect was not afforded to nonprofessional blacks.[3] Wells was also allowed to buy goods on credit at Menkens Department Store because of her profession.

During the summer, Wells took teacher-training classes at Fisk University and Lemoyne College to improve her classroom skills. It was while commuting from Memphis that she was forced from her first-class seat on the railroad, leading to her unsuccessful lawsuit. Her first experience with harsh racism would direct her life into civil-rights activism.

Soon after Ida Wells arrived in Memphis, her Aunt Fannie moved to California, taking Annie and Lily Wells

This picture of a Fisk University class was taken around the time that Ida B. Wells attended.

with her. It was another major change in Wells's life. For the first time she was alone without family support or responsibilities. Wells still had to support her sisters financially, and she sent money to Aunt Fannie in California. She was now earning sixty dollars a month as a teacher, but she struggled to meet all of her obligations. She sent ten dollars for the support of her sisters, and she also helped her brothers, George and Jim, who needed expense money as they worked as apprentices. Wells had to pay rent to the families with whom she was staying, and in the summer when school was out, she had no income at all. Even during the school year, teachers' salaries were late or sometimes only partially paid when the school board ran out of money.

Still, being in Memphis was an exciting and fulfilling time for the bright young woman. She was at last able to take part in the social and intellectual life of a busy city. She joined a lyceum, meeting every Friday afternoon in the Christian church. A lyceum was an organization that offered lectures, recitations, debates, and music. Wells described the experiences as "a breath of life to me."[4] The afternoon always ended with a reading of the *Evening Star*, a journal put out by the lyceum describing upcoming events and news from the Memphis African-American community. The *Evening Star* contained poetry and a feature called "They Say," which allowed local people to give their opinions.

When the editor of the *Evening Star* had a chance to return to his previous job, he left. The newspaper was now without an editor, and the lyceum members searched for a replacement. During the weekly meetings, Ida Wells had impressed many of the members with her bright mind and her ability to express herself. But Wells had no idea she was making such a good impression; so when the job of editor was offered to her, she admitted it was "to my great surprise."[5] Ida Wells was a young woman in her mid-twenties from a small country town. Her only job experience was in teaching elementary school. She certainly did not expect a job as editor of even a small newspaper.

Ida Wells took the job and was determined to keep the paper lively and interesting. She found that she enjoyed the work immensely. She liked to write more than she liked to teach school. A seed was planted in her mind that would quickly bloom.

Among the people who came to the lyceum meetings was the Reverend R. N. Countee, editor of a Baptist weekly, *The Living Way*. He began to notice Wells's short pieces in the *Evening Star*. Countee was the pastor of a leading Baptist church in Memphis. When he told Ida Wells that he liked her articles in the *Evening Star* so much that he wanted to reprint them in his weekly, it was a great compliment. Then he invited Wells to write articles regularly for *The Living Way*.

Wells wrote about how she had been dragged from her seat on the train, and she wrote many articles that she hoped would be helpful to the African-American community. She knew that many black people had very little education, so she wrote her articles as simply as she could. "I never used a word of two syllables where one would serve the purpose," she later wrote.[6]

At the beginning of her writing career, Ida Wells decided not to use her real name, but instead used the pen name, "Iola." Her close friends knew who Iola was, but the general reading public did not. Wells believed she could write with more freedom by using a pen name.

Ida Wells was not only enjoying her new writing career, but she was having fun in her social life. She belonged to an active circle of young black men and women who played games like checkers and Parcheesi (a game similar to backgammon, played on a board with checkers and dice). They went horseback riding and attended basketball games, concerts, and dramatic readings. Although Wells was popular with the young men in the group, she was not eager to settle down. She enjoyed the dramatic presentations so much that she organized a new dramatic club. As she played roles in these plays, Wells improved her own speaking ability.

Many of the teachers with whom Wells associated

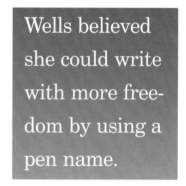

Wells believed she could write with more freedom by using a pen name.

came from wealthier backgrounds than she did. They lived in nice homes and dressed in the latest fashions. Wells wanted to fit in with her friends at the social activities, but nice clothing was expensive, and she had little money to spare. The other black women came to the functions in silks, brocades, satin, and velvet, with jewelry of diamonds and pearls. Wells could not afford such things. She bought clothing on credit at Menkens Department Store and then struggled with the payments. She would see something she liked and buy it, then scold herself for wasting money. "Bought a hat costing $3.50," she lamented once, "that I am sorry for now."[7] To solve her problem, she sometimes bought cheaper dresses and then sewed on lace and other fancy trimmings to make the garment look more expensive.

Ida Wells was very active in the A.M.E. Church, teaching Sunday school and attending sermons by famous visiting clergymen. Wells attended the tent meetings when white revivalists brought Dwight Moody and when Ira D. Sankey came to Memphis. At the time, black preachers were coming to black churches on Sunday and saying things Ida Wells had never heard before. For the first time in her life, Wells heard men of her own race thundering against the way white people treated black people. One of the preachers she heard was Bishop Henry McNeal Turner, who was urging black people to emigrate to Africa, where they could live with dignity.[8]

Bishop Turner

Henry McNeal Turner was born in 1833 in South Carolina. His grandfather had been brought to America as a slave, but he demanded his freedom. He said there was an English law forbidding the enslavement of a person with royal blood. Turner's grandfather was the descendant of an African king. Henry McNeal Turner was born free, but he suffered discrimination, as all African-American men did at the time.

CIVIL RIGHTS.

THE OUTRAGE OF THE SUPREME COURT
OF THE UNITED STATES UPON THE
BLACK MAN.

REVIEWED IN A REPLY TO THE NEW YORK "VOICE,"
THE GREAT TEMPERANCE PAPER OF THE
UNITED STATES.

BY

BISHOP H. M. TURNER, D. D. LL.D.

Of the African Methodist Episcopal Church.

PRICE TEN CENTS.
To Cover Expense of Printing.

PUBLISHED IN PAMPHLET FORM BY REQUEST.

Turner became a preacher in the A.M.E. Church at the age of twenty, and he became

Above is the cover page of Henry McNeal Turner's paper, *Civil Rights*.

a bishop at the age of forty-seven. During the Civil War, he was appointed by President Abraham Lincoln to be the first black chaplain to black troops in the U.S. Army. He was awarded a Doctor of Literature from the University of Pennsylvania and a Doctor of Divinity from Wilberforce University. Bishop Turner was eloquent and brilliant, and his articles appeared often in *Harpers Weekly* and other national magazines.

Ida Wells was soon writing for other black newspapers around the country. They had seen the articles by "Iola," and they liked them. Many newspapers wanted to reprint her articles. Because of this growing recognition and her social life, Wells was happy in Memphis. "I had made a very pleasant place for myself in the life of Memphis," she later wrote.[9] But her life was soon to take another turn. Her contented world would be shaken.

> "I had made a very pleasant place for myself in the life of Memphis."

Aunt Fannie was living out in California with her own three children and Ida Wells's two sisters, and she was unhappy. She wrote a letter to Wells, asking her to come to Visalia, California, where she was living. Aunt Fannie wanted her niece to get a teaching job in Visalia and help with the care of the children.

Ida Wells knew that asking Aunt Fannie to cope with five children was unfair, but she didn't want to leave Memphis and the life she had there. She was grateful to Aunt Fannie for all she had done for her and felt she owed her something. Ida Wells felt like she was being pulled in two directions.

At that time, the National Education Association, a teacher's group, was sponsoring a trip west for teachers. Wells decided to join the group on the trip, which ended up in California. At least she could visit Aunt Fannie. Wells traveled through Kansas, Colorado, and Utah. She wrote articles about the trip and sent them back to *The*

Living Way. Wells had a round-trip ticket, and she had every intention of returning to Memphis after seeing her aunt. But when Wells reached Visalia, Aunt Fannie was insistent. She convinced Wells to sell her return ticket and to see the superintendent of schools in Visalia about a permanent teaching job.

Ida Wells was trapped in a situation she did not like. She was hired in Visalia and sent to a broken-down one-room schoolhouse with eighteen students. This was the entire population of black children in the town. Up on the hills was a nice school building where white, American Indian, and Mexican students were taught. Wells was told that the black families of Visalia had asked that their children be taught in a separate school. Wells felt that by teaching black students separately in an inferior school she was supporting something she hated—segregation and discrimination.

Ida Wells was deeply unhappy in Visalia, but she did not know how to escape the situation. Her aunt pleaded with her to stay and help with the five children, including Wells's two sisters. Wells argued with Aunt Fannie, trying to explain that she was a young woman who needed more opportunities than Visalia had to offer. Finally, Aunt Fannie issued a demand. Either Ida Wells would stay in Visalia and help with the children, or she would have to take her two sisters with her to Memphis when she left. Aunt Fannie simply could not handle five children.

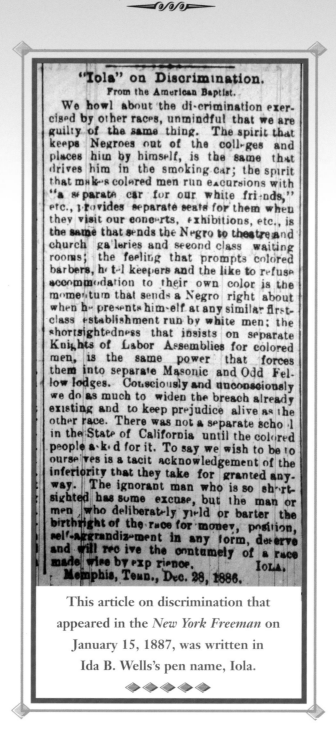

"Iola" on Discrimination.

From the American Baptist.

We howl about the discrimination exercised by other races, unmindful that we are guilty of the same thing. The spirit that keeps Negroes out of the colleges and places him by himself, is the same that drives him in the smoking car; the spirit that makes colored men run excursions with "a separate car for our white friends," etc., provides separate seats for them when they visit our concerts, exhibitions, etc., is the same that sends the Negro to theatre and church galleries and second class waiting rooms; the feeling that prompts colored barbers, hotel keepers and the like to refuse accommodation to their own color is the momentum that sends a Negro right about when he presents himself at any similar first-class establishment run by white men; the shortsightedness that insists on separate Knights of Labor Assemblies for colored men, is the same power that forces them into separate Masonic and Odd Fellow lodges. Consciously and unconsciously we do as much to widen the breach already existing and to keep prejudice alive as the other race. There was not a separate school in the State of California until the colored people asked for it. To say we wish to be to ourselves is a tacit acknowledgement of the inferiority that they take for granted anyway. The ignorant man who is so shortsighted has some excuse, but the man or men who deliberately yield or barter the birthright of the race for money, position, self-aggrandizement in any form, deserve and will receive the contumely of a race made wise by experience.   IOLA.

Memphis, Tenn., Dec. 28, 1886.

This article on discrimination that appeared in the *New York Freeman* on January 15, 1887, was written in Ida B. Wells's pen name, Iola.

Having no money for the return trip to Memphis, Wells wrote to friends asking for their help. When she received enough money as a loan, she prepared to leave with her sisters. However, fourteen-year-old Annie refused to go with her. Annie was too attached to her cousin, Aunt Fannie's daughter, who was near her own age. As a result, only Ida Wells and eleven-year-old Lily left for Memphis.

When Wells returned to Memphis, she didn't feel as happy as she thought she would. She wrote in her diary that she did not understand what was wrong with her. "My life seems awry," she wrote, describing "fits of loneliness."[10]

Most of Ida Wells's friends and fellow teachers were getting married and starting their own families. Ida herself had suitors, but she would often drive them away by arguing with them or winning games against them. It seemed she was deliberately ruining her own chances for romance. In the winter of 1887, twenty-five-year-old Ida Wells was the only unmarried lady left in the building where she taught.

Ida Wells had never taught above the fourth-grade level, and this was another reason she was unhappy. She wanted to teach older students. She described the "monotony of primary work," calling it "distasteful."[11] Wells was beginning to realize she did not like teaching all that much, yet she still did her work conscientiously.[12] On the other hand, Wells was enjoying her writing career more and more. She now knew that her true vocation lay not in teaching but in journalism. Wells later wrote that her writing gave her the chance to express "the real 'me.'"[13]

Chapter 5

"The Brilliant Iola"

While Ida Wells resumed her teaching career in Memphis, her journalistic work became even more important in her life. The Reverend William J. Simmons of American Baptist Home Missions and editor for the Negro Press Association was on his way through Memphis. He asked to meet "the brilliant Iola" whose work he had read in so many black newspapers.

When Simmons did meet with Wells, he invited her to write articles for the *American Baptist* newspaper. He offered Wells payment of one dollar a week for her work. This was the first time anyone had paid Wells anything for her writing. The biggest problem that kept Wells from following her dream of becoming a full-time journalist was that it just did not pay enough. In fact, it paid almost nothing.

Simmons invited Wells to attend the National Press Association convention in Louisville, Kentucky. This was an organization for black writers. When Wells attended in 1889, she met several famous African Americans, including orator Frederick Douglass and a former U.S. senator from Mississippi, Blanche K. Bruce. Bruce had become one of many African-American politicians elected to office in the South after the Civil War, only to be swept out when conditions changed. Wells was elected secretary of the National Press Association at the convention. Simmons continued to encourage Wells in her writing. Years later, he was one of the people she credited for her success.

Ida Wells was now writing articles that appeared all over the United States. T. Thomas Fortune, editor of the *New York Age*, an influential black newspaper, praised Ida Wells for her brilliant mind. Wells continued to write for *The Living Way*, usually articles of local interest, such as social events and concert reviews. But sometimes she wrote a hard-hitting article that focused on the abuses of the civil rights of black people. When Wells learned of the unjust treatment of a black person, she covered it in the newspaper. Her articles were regularly reprinted in such newspapers as the *Detroit Plain Dealer*, the *Indianapolis World*, the *Chattanooga Justice*, and the *Kansas City Gate Press*—all black newspapers with good circulation. The circulation of a newspaper is measured by the number of copies sold.

Thomas T. Fortune praised Ida B. Wells for her hard-hitting newspaper commentaries.

Although she was dubbed "the Princess of the Press"[2] as her fame spread, Wells still needed to teach to make a living. Except for the dollar she was earning from the *American Baptist*, she received nothing else but free newspaper subscriptions and free copies of the papers in which her work appeared.

Ida Wells had grown weary of teaching, especially since she remained in the primary grades. To make matters worse, conditions in the black schools of Memphis were very difficult. As with black schools all over the South at the time, the Memphis schools were crowded and substandard. Most were two-room frame buildings without decent ventilation in the summer or heating in the winter. Wells usually taught about seventy students. Every summer she took part in teacher institutes to improve her teaching skills.

Ida Wells was always trying to better herself, so she

Freedom's Journal

The first black newspaper ever published in the United States appeared in 1827. It was co-edited by Samuel E. Cornish, a product of New York's famous African Free School, and John B. Russworm, black America's first college graduate. The newspaper *Freedom's Journal* called for freedom for African-American slaves, and for full civil and political rights for all blacks in the nation. The newspaper consisted of four tabloid-size pages. This is about one-half the size of a regular newspaper page.

took elocution lessons to improve her speaking voice. (Elocution is the art of public speaking.) She learned what tone of voice to use at different times. She also learned gestures that were useful in gaining the attention of listeners. Sometimes Wells recited dramatic scenes from plays like *MacBeth* at local concerts.

In addition to all the articles she wrote, Ida Wells wrote short stories. She dreamed of writing a novel. She kept a notebook in which she jotted down ideas for later use in the book she would write. The need to make money was always on her mind. If she made money doing something other than teaching, she would be free to write more. Wells even thought about buying a chicken farm with her brothers, George and James. The chicken farm might have been profitable enough to free her from the need to teach.

In 1889, twenty-seven-year-old Ida Wells was asked to become editor and partner of the *Free Speech and Headlight* (later called *Free Speech*), a small Memphis newspaper that was published once a week. Wells's sharp criticisms of local black leaders who she thought were failing the black community had attracted the attention of the Reverend F. Nightingale, the publisher of *Free Speech*.[3]

Wells agreed to join the newspaper only if she had some control over the content. As a result, she received a one-third interest in the newspaper, which she bought with her hard-earned savings. That meant she would get one third of the profits the newspaper earned. Wells became the editor, Nightingale the sales manager, and J. L. Fleming the business manager. At last, Wells was getting close to earning money for her writing, but she was not yet making serious money. She had to continue teaching until the newspaper sold enough copies to make a good profit.

Wells continued to write under the pen name Iola. She had liked the sound of the name when she had chosen it, and she felt the need to use a pen name to create a slight barrier between her writing and herself. Many of her articles were sharp and critical, and although many knew who Iola was, many others did not.

Ida Wells felt strongly about the conditions of the black schools in Memphis. She wanted to write an article exposing the problems so something would be done to correct them. Because she still depended upon her salary

Ida B. Wells-Barnett (center) was very close to her two sisters, Annie (left) and Lily. Here are the three of them pictured later in life.

from the Memphis School Board, she asked the Reverend Nightingale to sign the article. Even using her pen name of Iola would not shield her from possible retaliation from the school board.

Believing the Reverend Nightingale would sign the article, Ida Wells wrote about the Memphis schools. She described abuses she had seen firsthand. She denounced the broken-down buildings and the poor skills of many of her fellow teachers. These teachers had no ability in the classroom, but they were hired because of their friendships with people on the school board. Wells made a special point of noting that while white schools received high funding, the black schools were denied the money they needed and, as a result, the black children suffered.[4]

Since Wells had made such serious charges against the school board that was employing her, she knew she would be in serious trouble if the story came out under her true name or her pen name. But just before the article went to press, Reverend Nightingale changed his mind and refused to sign it. Wells now had to either scrap the article or admit to being its author. She knew she was jeopardizing her job, but she decided to go ahead and publish it. She did so "in the interest of the children of our race."[5] This decision was a daring act of courage.

When the Memphis School Board met to elect teachers for the next school year, Ida B. Wells, successful teacher for seven years, was not rehired. She went to the board for an explanation. A copy of the newspaper containing her article was shown to her. The board could no longer employ a teacher who had called such attention to their shortcomings. It was too late in the year for Wells to find a teaching job in another district. She was not surprised at what had happened. She had known that publishing the article would probably cost her the teaching position.

Ida Wells was now dependent on her journalism for her livelihood. In order to improve the profits of the newspaper and increase her income, she went on a sales trip. She traveled all around the Mississippi River Valley from Arkansas to Tennessee and Mississippi, promoting the *Free Speech*. It was unusual to see a young woman like Wells traveling alone and giving sales pitches for anything, so she was an object of interest. Her enthusiasm won friends. She spoke at social meetings, clubs, and conventions. Whenever she saw a gathering of people, she joined in to talk about the newspaper. Wells visited large and small towns, asking for subscriptions. She also recruited local people who promised to keep their eyes and ears open for stories she might use. She wanted to hear about instances of racism in their areas, and she promised to publicize them in her newspaper.

At Greenville, Mississippi, Wells

> Whenever she saw a gathering of people, she joined in to talk about the newspaper.

spoke to a group of lawyers, and when she had finished, every single man there ordered a subscription. She was so loaded down with silver dollars that she had to struggle to get to the bank and make the deposit. After nine months of vigorously promoting *Free Speech*, Wells had increased its circulation from fifteen hundred to four thousand subscribers. Wells was now earning only ten dollars a month less than she had earned as a Memphis schoolteacher, and she was doing something she loved—talking to people and writing about things that were important to them.

As Ida Wells traveled around the South getting subscribers, she discovered the status of black people was going down dramatically. During several decades after the Civil War, black people had gained the rights of citizenship. Remarkable things happened, such as blacks being elected to high office in the South. But in 1890, Mississippi revised the state constitution, which had granted new rights to freedmen. Other southern states were doing the same. The earlier constitution had given black men the right to vote, but the new constitution took that right away.

Ida Wells recalled that when she was a little girl, she had watched her father marching proudly off to the polling place on Election Day to cast his vote. Her father could buy a glass of beer at the Holly Springs saloon and drink it alongside his white neighbors. When Elizabeth Wells, her mother, wanted to have a church picnic, she simply reserved a day at the Holly Springs park for herself

Jim Crow Segregation Laws

The freedmen who had enjoyed new citizenship rights after the Civil War now found those rights disappearing. Segregation and discrimination laws were passed, denying black people equality. These laws were called Jim Crow laws. The origin of the term "Jim Crow" is not clear. In 1832, Thomas D. Rice wrote a song and dance called Jim Crow. The name was then applied to laws and customs that segregated black people.

By 1877, African Americans in the South were forced into separate and unequal accommodations in schools, transportation systems, and public places. They had to sit in the back of theaters, restaurants, and even churches. They were often barred entirely from parks and hotels. Even city cemeteries were closed to African-American dead. As new white state governments in the South took away what the federal government had guaranteed to African Americans, the federal government did nothing.

> She had *Free Speech* printed on pink paper so even those who could not read would know the difference.

and the other parishioners. But none of this was possible anymore. New laws were enacted to keep black men from voting. Black people could not eat or drink with white neighbors. The park was closed to black events.

Seeing this dramatic loss of African-American civil rights stirred Ida Wells to an even more active role in using her newspaper to fight against injustice. She was ever alert to efforts to reduce the influence of *Free Speech*. When some white men began selling the *Police Gazette* to illiterate blacks, telling them it was *Free Speech*, Wells acted swiftly. She had *Free Speech* printed on pink paper so even those who could not read would know the difference. Many blacks who were not able to read still bought the paper and took it home to their families, where children or friends could read it to them, as Ida Wells herself had read the newspaper to her father and his friends.

Ida B. Wells wanted to do even more than publish her activist newspaper. When *New York Age* publisher T. Thomas Fortune created the Afro-American League in 1887, the intent was to fight for African-American civil rights through the courts. The league also declared war on the crime of lynching, harassment of African-American voters in the South, the convict-lease system that led to abuse of African-American prisoners, and racial discrimination of all kinds.[6] In 1891, Wells attended the Afro-American League convention in Knoxville, Tennessee, where she presented a paper on what the black women of the South could do to improve conditions.

Ida Wells was on another trip getting subscriptions for the *Free Speech* in 1892 when terrible news reached her from Memphis. There had been a lynching, and Thomas Moss, one of her closest Memphis friends, was dead. Under normal constitutional laws, a person cannot be punished for a crime until he or she receives a fair trial. Lynching deprives the accused of that fair trial. In most lynchings, a large group of people captured and killed someone, often by hanging, shooting, or even burning the person alive.

The lynching of Moss dramatically changed the focus of Wells's crusade. She continued to fight for African-American civil rights, but the crime of lynching occupied her mind and heart.

Chapter 6

Outrage in Memphis

I da B. Wells was one of the many black people in
Memphis who knew and liked Thomas Moss—
"Tommie" to his friends. Wells later wrote: "He and
his wife Betty were the best friends I had in town."[1]
Thomas and Betty Moss were the parents of one daughter,
Maurine, and they were expecting a second child. Wells
was Maurine's godmother. Thomas Moss was a mail carrier
who, with his friends Calvin McDowell and Henry
Stewart, had opened a grocery store called The People's
Grocery. The store was located in a racially mixed neighborhood at a place called the curve because the streetcar
turned sharply at that point. Moss did his mail-carrying
job during the day; at night he usually went to the grocery
store to work on the business finances.

W. H. Barrett was a white grocer who owned a long-
established grocery store near the curve. For many years

he had done very good business with both black and white customers. When The People's Grocery opened in 1889, it offered competition, which Barrett resented. Before, Barrett's grocery store had been the only place to buy food. Now his black customers had a choice.

From the beginning, there was tension between Barrett and his friends and the owners of The People's Grocery. More and more black customers deserted the white man's store and shopped where they felt more comfortable. In March 1892, a fight broke out between some black and white boys who were playing a game of marbles near The People's Grocery. When the white boys appeared to be losing the fight, a white man stepped up and whipped one of the black boys. Soon the street filled with angry people of both races.

W. H. Barrett later claimed that a black man had attacked him. However, a black clerk at The People's Grocery said that Barrett had entered the store and pistol-whipped him. Events moved quickly after that. The white people eagerly seized on the violence to declare that The People's Grocery was a public nuisance that incited racial violence. There was an outcry that the store must be closed. The white leaders of Memphis declared that the store had to be shut down at once.

Word spread in the black neighborhood that deputies were on the way to close down The People's Grocery. Friends of the owners armed themselves and prepared to

Lynching

The term "lynching" dates back to the late 1700s when Colonel Charles Lynch, a frontier judge and an officer in the American Revolutionary War, eliminated the need for trials and dispensed justice by sending accused people directly to the hangman. This type of justice came to be called lynching.

Lynching was never legal, but it was common in many parts of the country. Many people approved of it as a way to stop crime and keep the peace when the official law enforcement agencies did not appear effective. For example, in San Francisco in 1851 four men were hanged without legal trials. Horse thieves were commonly hanged from a handy tree without being arrested or convicted of their crimes.

Lynchings became tragically common in the American South, most often with black victims. Many efforts were made in the U.S. Congress to ban lynching by making it a federal crime. The House of Representatives passed many such bills, but they were always blocked in the U.S. Senate by southern senators. Almost five thousand people, primarily African Americans, were lynched in the United States between 1882 and 1968.[2] Of course, all lynchings were murders, because under the U.S. Constitution no person may be put to death without due process of law. No anti-lynching bill was ever passed, but in recent years when a person is victimized because of race or other specific characteristic, it is considered a hate crime and is a serious offense.

defend the store against what they considered an unfair attack. Not only did the local black people like the store, but they also respected the owners. Thomas Moss was literate and was president of The People's Grocery. McDowell and Stewart owned stock in the business and were part-time employees at the grocery store.

On a Saturday night at ten o'clock, Thomas Moss was working on the store's finances, as usual. Shots rang out from the rear of the store. Several white men had broken in, and the armed blacks fired on them, wounding three of them. The injured white men fled back onto the street and described what had happened. Soon reinforcements from the white community appeared. A large group of armed whites surged into The People's Grocery. Everyone in the store was taken into custody, along with many black men on the street. Meanwhile, the white mob poured into the unprotected grocery store and looted the shelves. Then the white mob roamed through the black neighborhood, breaking into homes, looting stores, and beating black residents.

On Sunday morning, the white newspapers of Memphis denounced the events of the past night as a full-scale black riot against white people. Groups of angry white men gathered at street corners to condemn the black men for shooting the whites who had broken into the back of the store. When the milling crowds of whites learned that the white men shot the night before would all survive, the black men standing near the jail to protect the black prisoners were relieved. Since no white man had died in the violence, the black people of Memphis thought tempers would cool and the men inside the jail would no longer be in danger.

However, on March 9, 1892, a group of white men were allowed to enter the jail where the black prisoners were being held. These white men believed that the main culprits in the entire affair were the owners of The People's Grocery, and so the white men took into custody Thomas Moss, Calvin McDowell, and Henry Stewart. The law enforcement officers in charge of the jail made no effort to prevent the removal of the three black men. The trio was loaded into a railroad car behind the jail, and the train carried them about a mile north of town.

There was no evidence that any of the three men had taken any part in the violence of the night when the white men were shot. In fact, Thomas Moss was working on the finances of the business, and McDowell was waiting on customers.

Witnesses later described what happened when the train stopped that night in the woods. Calvin McDowell fought for his life when he saw what was happening. He grabbed the handle of the pistol that was aimed at him and tried to wrest it from his attacker. They could not remove his clenched fingers from the handle of the gun, so they shot his hand to pieces, then killed him. Henry Stewart was shot to death. Thomas Moss pleaded for his life, saying he was the father of a small daughter and his wife was expecting another child soon. He was the only support of his family. Thomas Moss was also shot.

> Calvin McDowell grabbed the handle of the pistol that was aimed at him.

A full account of the manner in which the three men died appeared in the *Memphis Commercial*. A witness who was not identified described in detail how McDowell's hand was shot, and when the bodies were recovered, his right hand had indeed been mutilated by gunfire. This was proof that the witness who gave the account either saw it himself or talked to someone who did see it.

The black people of Memphis were outraged when they learned of the lynchings. Ida Wells returned to Memphis to be with the widowed Betty Moss and her daughter. Wells bought a pistol for protection. "One had better die fighting against injustice," she said, "than to die like a dog or a rat in a trap."[3] According to legend, after the killing of Moss and his companions, Wells usually walked the streets of Memphis with one or two pistols under her blouse or apron.[4]

Two weeks later, more than one thousand black people met in Memphis for a protest meeting. Wells was certain that the lynchers were well known to the authorities in

There were many lynchings of African Americans in the late 1800s and early 1900s. This picture of the 1920 lynching of Lige Daniels in Center, Texas, was turned into a sadistic postcard.

Memphis and were being protected from prosecution. What made the lynching of the three men so shocking was that they were well-respected businessmen, never involved in any criminal activities. Their only crime appeared to be that they were successful in competition with a white man. Reportedly, Thomas Moss's last words were: "Tell my people to go West—there is no justice for them here." Since no justice was forthcoming for the black people of Memphis, Ida Wells added her own words to those of her dear friend. "There is, therefore, only one thing left that we can do," she said. "Save our money and leave this town."[5] Wells urged all the black people who could to pick up their belongings and leave Memphis. Wells, along with many others, believed that lynching was now a tool for guaranteeing white supremacy in Memphis.[6]

The black population of Memphis at the time was about forty-four percent of the city.[7] Black people were a significant part of the Memphis economy, so the threat of many of them leaving was taken very seriously. Many blacks took Ida Wells's advice, leaving Memphis by the hundreds. Some crossed the Mississippi River into Arkansas. Two pastors, including Wells's old friend Reverend R. N. Countee, led their entire congregations west, leaving Memphis behind. Betty Moss remained in Memphis until the birth of her son, Thomas, Jr., and then she moved permanently to Indiana.

Oklahoma homesteaders rush to stake their claims to former American Indian lands in September 1891 during the Oklahoma land rush. White people in Memphis, Tennessee, were afraid that blacks would leave the city for the state of Oklahoma.

At the time, the U.S. government was opening up land in Oklahoma Frightened white businessmen in Memphis thought this land offer would entice even more blacks to leave, so white newspapers began a series of articles describing life in Oklahoma as terrible. Sensational stories described a brutal climate, deadly diseases, and hostile American Indians in the territory.[8] To counter this propaganda, Ida Wells traveled to Oklahoma and sent back favorable reports, which appeared in black newspapers. According to Wells, Oklahoma was an agreeable place to live.

White anger against Wells intensified as more black residents sold their homes in Memphis and moved away. Some of Wells's friends urged her to ease up on her campaign. Wells responded that she would not until justice was served for the Moss lynching. As for protecting herself against white violence, Wells said she was armed and ready for anything. "I felt if I could take one lyncher with me, this would even up the score a little bit."[9]

Blacks were leaving Memphis in droves by railroad, covered wagon and—if it was all they could manage—in uncovered wagons. Some even walked west.

Those black people who stayed behind in Memphis boycotted white businesses, further harming the economy of the city. They avoided riding the streetcars, walking to where they had to go. The Memphis Street Railroad was hit especially hard, and its superintendent visited Ida Wells and pleaded with her to ask black people to return to the trains. Wells told the man that three good men, friends of hers, had been lynched. As long as the whites in Memphis took no action against their killers, the boycott would continue.

White people in Memphis found it increasingly difficult to find domestic help. Entire blocks of homes in black neighborhoods stood empty. The boycott was having a dramatic impact, but there was no indication that the men who had lynched Thomas Moss and his companions would be punished.

In May 1892, Ida Wells went to a long-planned A.M.E. conference in Philadelphia and then traveled on to New York. She had left behind editorials for her newspaper. Many of the articles were on the subject of lynching and the reasons white people gave for committing this act of lawless violence. Ida Wells was hard-hitting and passionate in her opinions. Sometimes she dared to say things no other black writer had ever said before. She praised the black people of Georgetown, Kentucky, for setting fire to the town to retaliate for the lynching of a black man.[10] Many of her comments were considered highly inflammatory. She wrote that only when black people rose up in rage would "such outrages as lynching end."[11]

However, it was an editorial appearing on May 25, 1892, two months after the lynching of Moss and his companions, that caused the greatest fury in the white community of Memphis. Wells was in New York when the editorial was published. Wells commented on the most common justification used by white people for the lynching of black men—the need to protect white women from black attackers. While Wells admitted that some black men were indeed criminals who attacked both white and black women, she argued that many alleged rapes by black men against white women were not rapes. Wells said that some white women freely chose to be with black men. Since this relationship was condemned in the South, when a white woman and a black man were found together, the woman had no choice but to cry rape to protect herself from persecution. She could not admit the truth, which was that she and the black man loved one another. Had she admitted this truth, she would have become an outcast in her own community. Such comments had never been made before in print, and they created a firestorm in Memphis. It seemed to furious whites that Wells was damaging the reputation of white womanhood in the South.

> She wrote that only when black people rose up in rage would "such outrages as lynching end."

Ida Wells was meeting with T. Thomas Fortune, the publisher of *New York Age*, in New York City as the outcry against her rose up in Memphis. She'd had no idea that her words would make her an exile from the South.

Chapter 7

No Peace, No Justice

Thomas Fortune told Ida Wells that the white people of Memphis were so incensed at her editorial that violence had occurred. A mob had marched to the editorial offices of *Free Speech*, destroyed the printing equipment and furniture, and threatened death to anyone who resumed publishing the newspaper. According to one enraged Memphis resident, the author of the editorial Wells had written should be "brand[ed] . . . in the forehead with a hot iron."[1]

Wells's friends warned her not to return to Memphis. A gunman was said to be positioned at the railroad station in case she should return. She was told that if she appeared again in Memphis there would be a general bloodbath.[2]

Fortune offered Wells a position on the staff of the *New York Age*, and she accepted. Wells had courage and she wanted to return home, but she did not want to be the cause of violence that would bring harm to others besides herself. The first story she wrote for *New York Age* was a front-page exposé of lynching. She provided details, which were well-documented.

Wells challenged the common belief that it was poor, uneducated white people, outraged over some crime they believed a black person had committed, who usually carried out a lynching. She offered evidence that lynchings were more often the work of prominent white citizens, aided by local law enforcement. Wells wrote that most lynchings were strategies to keep blacks in an inferior status through fear and intimidation. For that reason, she refused to be at peace with the white establishment until there was justice for the black people.

Now exiled from the South, Wells was determined to tell the world the truth about lynching in the United States. She wrote that many white people in the South had never gotten over their resentment that blacks were no longer their property.

When African-American orator Frederick Douglass read the *New York Age* article by Wells, he came to New York to see her, praising her for her courage. Douglass and Wells became close friends.

In October 1892, Ida B. Wells launched her speaking career. The occasion was a testimonial dinner given on her behalf in Lyric Hall in New York by a group of black

Frederick Douglass

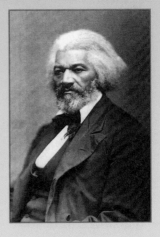

Frederick Douglass was born a slave in Maryland in 1818. He was brutally beaten by professional "slave-breaker" Edward Covey, who had been hired by Douglass's master to "tame" Douglass. This episode fired Douglass's determination to gain his freedom. While still a youth, he fled from slavery. As a freedman, he became one of America's greatest orators, and his accounts of slavery had a great impact on the country. Never before had there been a first-person account of slavery written with such eloquence. Douglass became a highly admired leader of black people.

women. About 250 black women from major eastern cities came to hear the thirty-year-old journalist talk about her experiences and her research. Wells was nervous speaking before such a large group of educated women. She was determined to be professional even as she related highly emotional material.

Wells described her firsthand research on the crime of lynching, often gained from talking to the relatives of victims. She gave the stark details of actual lynchings, which often involved torture and gory scenes. As Wells talked, tears began to roll down her face and she could not stop them. She was mortified that she had been unable to maintain her composure after trying so hard, but rather than hurting her message, her tears made it more powerful. The sight of a weeping young woman relating such terrible events deeply touched the ladies present. Her message was all the more profound because she showed such emotion. Wells's reputation as an outstanding speaker spread after her first speech in Lyric Hall.

In 1892, Wells published a pamphlet entitled *Southern Horrors: Lynch Law in All Its Phases*. In this pamphlet, she described what had happened to blacks in the South after the Civil War. True freedom did not come with freedom from slavery. The bonds of slavery were replaced by loss of rights and denial of due process of law. During slavery, the white masters terrorized their slaves with brutal repression. Now the freedman was terrorized by the threat of lynching.

Wells's fame spread throughout the United States, but the majority of her readers were African Americans. Wells wanted to reach white people in order to touch their consciences. They were the people with the power to improve the situation. During the Civil War, the cause of abolition had been taken up by sympathetic white people in the North, and that turned the tide of public opinion. Wells

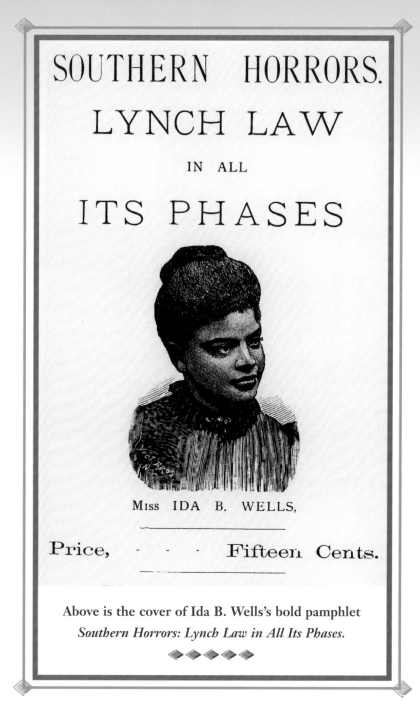

SOUTHERN HORRORS.

LYNCH LAW

IN ALL

ITS PHASES

Miss IDA B. WELLS,

Price, - - - - Fifteen Cents.

Above is the cover of Ida B. Wells's bold pamphlet
Southern Horrors: Lynch Law in All Its Phases.

hoped for the same thing to happen on the issue of lynching. So, to gain the attention of white America, Wells planned a speaking tour of Europe and the British Isles in 1893. She believed that if she received publicity for her cause overseas, the story would be picked up by the white American press. The trip was sponsored by the London-based National Anti-Lynching Committee and the Society for the Brotherhood of Man, a world organization working for just causes.

Ida Wells sailed on the *Teutonic* on April 5, 1893, bound for England. An English friend, Catherine Impey, accompanied her. Once they reached England, Impey would arrange for Wells's housing and plan her speaking tour. After docking in Liverpool, Wells was soon speaking to large groups of people in England and Scotland. She was scheduled to speak for fifteen minutes, but she so captivated the audience that she went on for twice that long, while men and women listened with rapt attention. In May, Wells addressed groups in Newcastle, Birmingham, and Manchester, England. The British newspapers gave Wells words of support. The *Birmingham Daily Post* of May 18, 1893, described Wells's address with glowing editorials.

Ida Wells succeeded in stirring up British opinion against the crime of lynching. Many of her audiences were shocked at her stories. When asked by one group if American blacks had not tried to introduce anti-lynching laws in the United States, Wells told the dismal story of such efforts. Blacks approaching Congress were rebuffed. When an anti-lynching group of African Americans asked for permission to address a meeting of U.S. governors, they were told they could not see the governors. They were told to present their petitions to the doorkeepers of the building. When the British audience heard this, some cried, "Shame!"[3]

Wells sailed home on the *New York*, and enjoyed the trip immensely. Very few white Americans were on the ship, but there was a party of young white Englishmen. Some of them belonged to the Society of Friends (Quakers). This group had a long history of opposing slavery before the Civil War and fighting all kinds of injustice. Wells found them friendly, and she was delighted that they did not seem to care what color her skin was.

> Many of her audiences were shocked at her stories.

Upon her return to the United States, Ida Wells attended the 1893 World's Columbian Exposition in Chicago, which commemorated the four-hundredth anniversary of the discovery of America by Christopher Columbus. The exposition had 150 buildings on 666 acres along Lake Michigan. Twenty-two million people attended the event. Wells took note of the fact that African Americans were excluded from planning the exposition and from officially participating in any of the events.

Ida Wells wrote the pamphlet: *"The Reason Why the Colored American Is Not in the World's Columbian Exposition."* The pamphlet described how the exclusion was another example of the "oppression put upon the colored people in this land of the free and the home of the brave."[4]

There was some black representation at the Columbian Exposition in the form of an exhibit featuring the nation of Haiti. Haiti, like many other countries, had a building there, and they chose Frederick Douglass as the director. He had been the U.S. consul general to Haiti in 1889. Without Haiti's exhibit, there would have been no black presence at all. During the three months of the exposition, Douglass gave Ida Wells a desk in the Haitian exhibit. She passed out her pamphlets there. Ten thousand copies were circulated.

Wells noted that even though blacks were officially excluded from the exposition, the Haitian building was one of the most popular attractions with white visitors. They were fascinated by black culture and eager to meet Frederick Douglass personally. Wells observed how many white people lined up to shake hands with the black orator.

One day Douglass invited Wells to lunch at the Boston Oyster House, a popular lunchroom in Chicago. Wells reminded Douglass that blacks were not served there, but Douglass insisted on going anyway. At the time, although there were no laws segregating public places in the North, frequently black patrons were not served at restaurants.

The managers of the establishments hoped the black patrons would get the message when no waiter came to take their order. They hoped the black customers would quietly leave, and they usually did.

When Ida Wells and Frederick Douglass walked in, the waiters did not give them menus or offer to seat them. Douglass selected a table for Wells and himself, and after seating Wells, Douglass also sat down. At that moment, the owner of the restaurant recognized Douglass. The atmosphere changed immediately. The owner was cordial to Douglass and Wells, and the waiter hurried to take their orders. It was obvious that a well-known African American like Douglass would be accorded courtesy and service to avoid bad publicity, but for the average black patron there would be no service. It was a sad reminder to Douglass and Wells just what ordinary people of their race faced, day after day.

Ida Wells decided not to return to New York and to make Chicago her new home instead. She had met Ferdinand Barnett, the publisher of a large black newspaper, *The Chicago Conservator*, at the Columbian Exposition. They became friends, and Barnett offered Wells a job at his newspaper, which she accepted. Barnett had already heard a great deal about Ida Wells, and he found her passion for justice appealing.

Ferdinand Barnett was a prominent, successful attorney in Chicago, as well as the owner of the newspaper. He

Ferdinand Barnett was a former slave who became a successful lawyer and newspaper owner.

was the son of slaves who had purchased their freedom and moved to Canada, raising their children as free people.

Barnett had been a high school teacher in Missouri as a young man, then he moved to Chicago to study law. After graduating from law school in 1878, he practiced law, and then in 1882 established *The Chicago Conservator*. Barnett married Mary Graham of Ontario, Canada, who was the first black woman to graduate from the University of Michigan. Mary Barnett died in 1888, leaving two small children— Ferdinand, who was four, and Albert, who was two. Barnett's mother took over the care of the children.

Like Ida Wells, Ferdinand Barnett was active in promoting civil rights. He was an official of the National Conference of Colored Men, which promoted race unity and worked against discriminatory practices. He was also president of The Colored Men's Library Association and, like Wells, was vocally critical of whites who favored a few prominent blacks while acting to keep the majority of black people in second-class citizenship.

Ida Wells and Ferdinand Barnett began to date, and their relationship quickly became serious. In March 1894, Wells was planning a second trip overseas. Before she left, Barnett proposed marriage to her. Wells promised to marry him when she returned from her speaking trip. All during her journey through the British Isles, Wells received many beautiful love letters from Barnett.

Ida Wells spoke to large audiences in Liverpool and London. She delivered ten addresses in Liverpool. Her audiences for each averaged about one thousand people. She was now comfortable addressing large groups. News of her speaking tour received good coverage in the United States, arousing the anger of some newspapers in the South. *The Memphis Daily Commercial* complained about Wells's telling horror stories of lynchings in Memphis and holding the city up to public scorn all over the world. But this very newspaper had described grisly crimes against black people. They had related an incident on May 23, 1893, when a black man was taken from jail, kicked and slashed, then hanged from a telegraph pole. He was burned as the mob looked on.

While overseas, Wells also contributed to the *Chicago Inter-Ocean*, a black newspaper. She detailed her activities and opinions in a column entitled "Ida B. Wells Abroad." During her four months in England, she believed she had finally aroused the consciences of many white people, both in the British Isles and in the United States.

Prominent white people in the United States often justified lynching as the only way to deal with black crime. They were not ashamed of holding these views. Gradually, due to Wells's campaign, it was

> A black man was taken from jail, kicked and slashed, then hung from a telegraph pole.

more difficult to hold such opinions. Condemnations of lynching began to come from southern political and religious leaders who had previously kept silent. Clergymen were denouncing lynching from the pulpits of white churches. The cloak of respectability that had long sheltered the crime of lynching from condemnation was falling away. By shining a glaring light on the horrors of lynching, Wells made it very hard for anybody to defend it. This was exactly what she had hoped to do.

On July 24, 1894, Ida B. Wells returned to New York and immediately received offers to speak all over the United States. She traveled to Philadelphia and spoke on the same platform as Frederick Douglass. She returned to Chicago in August and spoke to the Ida B. Wells Club, a Chicago group of black women united against racism. Wells had formed the club as a way for black women to help the cause of justice. Wells Clubs were being formed all over the United States.

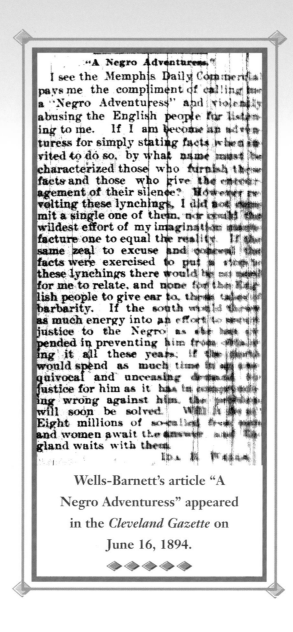

"A Negro Adventuress."

I see the Memphis Daily Commercial pays me the compliment of calling me a "Negro Adventuress" and violently abusing the English people for listening to me. If I am become an adventuress for simply stating facts when invited to do so, by what name must be characterized those who furnish these facts and those who give the encouragement of their silence? However revolting these lynchings, I did not commit a single one of them, nor could the wildest effort of my imagination manufacture one to equal the reality. If the same zeal to excuse and conceal the facts were exercised to put a stop to these lynchings there would be no need for me to relate, and none for the English people to give ear to, these tales of barbarity. If the south would throw as much energy into an effort to secure justice to the Negro as she has expended in preventing him from obtaining it all these years; if the north would spend as much time in an unequivocal and unceasing demand for justice for him as it has in committing wrong against him, the problem will soon be solved. With it all Eight millions of so-called free men and women await the answer and England waits with them.

IDA B. WELLS.

Wells-Barnett's article "A Negro Adventuress" appeared in the *Cleveland Gazette* on June 16, 1894.

Wells spent the remainder of the year speaking all around the country. At a huge meeting in Providence, Rhode Island, she again shared the speaker's platform with Frederick Douglass. Wells never saw her old friend after that engagement in November of 1894. Frederick Douglass died on February 20, 1895. Wells led a memorial service for him in San Francisco, California, where she had been speaking.

Chapter 8

"Brave Woman!"

n June 27, 1895, thirty-two-year-old Ida Bell Wells married thirty-eight-year-old Ferdinand Lee Barnett. The wedding took place at 8:00 P.M. on Thursday in Bethel Church. Annie and Lily Wells were the bridesmaids, wearing lemon crepe dresses. Ida Wells walked down the aisle in a white satin dress trimmed in chiffon and orange blossoms. The church was filled to capacity, and outside on the street, the crowd was so thick that the wedding carriage had difficulty taking the bride and groom away after the ceremony.

Wells-Barnett wrote in her diary: "I was married in the city of Chicago to Attorney F. L. Barnett, and retired to what I thought was the privacy of a home."[1] However, one week after the wedding, Ida Wells-Barnett became editor of *The Chicago Conservator.* She immediately produced her strongest condemnation of lynching ever in a pamphlet entitled *A Red Record. Tabulated Statistics and Alleged Causes of Lynching in the United States.* Frederick Douglass had written the preface shortly before he died. He wrote: "Brave woman! You have done your people and mine a service which can neither be weighed nor measured."[2]

All the events described in the pamphlet were taken from the work of white journalists and first appeared in the *Chicago Tribune* in 1894. The statistics were based on the year 1893, when 197 people—primarily black Americans—were lynched in the United States. Some were lynched after being accused of a serious crime, such as murder, arson, or rape. Others were lynched for relatively minor offenses, such as petty thievery, or just for being impolite to white people. Five were lynched for no apparent offense, except that the black victim had somehow aroused the anger of a white person. Alabama led with the most lynchings.

Wells-Barnett gave vivid details of individual lynchings, describing how the victims died. She told of one black man—Hamp Biscoe—who was lynched in England, Arkansas. Biscoe was known to be mentally ill and suspicious of outsiders. He was about to lose his farm through foreclosure. When he saw deputies approaching the house, he believed they were coming to evict him and his family. Biscoe fired at the deputies, wounding one of them. The

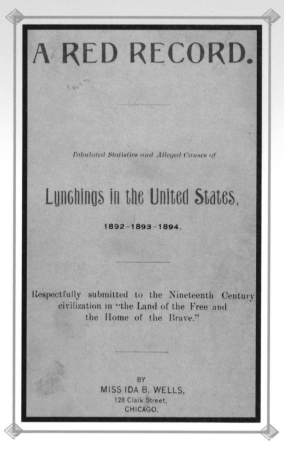

A RED RECORD.

Tabulated Statistics and Alleged Causes of

Lynchings in the United States,

1892-1893-1894.

Respectfully submitted to the Nineteenth Century civilization in "the Land of the Free and the Home of the Brave."

BY
MISS IDA B. WELLS,
128 Clark Street,
CHICAGO.

In *A Red Record*, Ida B. Wells-Barnett listed statistics and alleged excuses for lynchings in the United States.

deputy was not seriously injured, and he later recovered. But Biscoe had sealed his fate by firing a gun at a white deputy.

A group of armed white men shot Biscoe and his wife, who was pregnant at the time and had a young baby in her arms. The wounded Biscoes, along with their thirteen-year-old son and the baby, were taken to a nearby house and held there. What happened then was witnessed by the teenage boy who, though fatally wounded, lived long enough to tell his story. He saw the men shoot his parents, killing them. When the boy tried to flee the house, he too was shot. He lay on the floor, pretending to be dead. He saw the men rob his parents' dead bodies. He was shot a second time, but when the crackles of gunfire attracted the attention of neighbors who came, the boy was able to tell what had happened.[3]

In Roseland, Louisiana, another black man—Meredith Lewis—had been accused of murder but was acquitted by a white jury. The local white people did not like the verdict. They came to the jail, seized Lewis, and lynched him. In Knox Point, Louisiana, some white farmers noticed they were missing some of their hogs. They immediately suspected two black neighbors. The black men protested that they were their innocent, but they were taken out and hanged by a mob.

In Moberly, Missouri, and Fort Madison, South Carolina, black men were lynched for the crime of being "saucy to white people."[4] The men had apparently failed to observe the custom of leaving the sidewalk and walking in the gutter when white pedestrians approached.

The lynch law was so commonly applied in the South that sometimes there did not have to be any reason at all. Black people could be lynched just because white people wanted to lynch them. "Parties of men who had it in their power to kill them, and who chose to avenge some fancied wrong by murder," Wells-Barnett wrote, "could simply do so by bypassing the court."[5]

After Ida Wells-Barnett married, she and her husband moved into their new home, along with her two sisters, Annie and Lily. They all lived together until the sisters married and moved away. Ferdinand Barnett's mother and his two young sons lived in a house nearby, and his mother remained the caretaker for the boys.

The Barnetts hired a housekeeper, and she and Ferdinand Barnett did all the household chores. Ferdinand Barnett enjoyed cooking, but his wife did not. In fact, she did not care for any domestic work, and her husband accepted that.

The personalities of the Barnetts complemented each other very well. Many years later, daughter Alfreda Duster described her father as "a very mild-mannered man, he was not aggressive . . . or outspoken like my mother."[6]

Although Ida Wells-Barnett admitted in her autobiography that she was not as eager as some women were to have children, she became the mother of Charles Aked Barnett on March 25, 1896.[7] The child was named for a very dear friend, Charles Aked.

Motherhood was rewarding for Ida Wells-Barnett. She was delighted with her son. She approached her new role as a mother with the same enthusiasm she invested in writing. Still, she was determined to continue her work against lynching. She would not let motherhood interfere with her travels, but she insisted on nursing her baby. When Charles was four months old, Wells-Barnett took him to a Washington meeting of the Association of Colored Women's Clubs. A nurse came along to help with the baby while his mother was speaking from the podium. The

Reverend Aked of Liverpool

Reverend Charles F. Aked was a popular and dynamic young minister in Liverpool. When Ida Wells-Barnett was in Liverpool, she heard him preach at his church, Pembroke Chapel. She was so impressed with his passion and sincerity that she shared with him her crusade to end lynching in the United States. Aked became her ally, allowing her to address his congregation, and he soon becoming leader of the British anti-lynching movement. Aked and his wife hosted Wells while she was in the British Isles and offered their home as her headquarters.

delegates were delighted with the baby, naming him The Baby of the Federation.

Wells-Barnett traveled to many cities in the United States with her baby. Once, when he was about six months old, she left him sleeping with the nurse. Charles awoke to hear his mother's voice speaking from the podium. He could not understand why she did not come when he cried. Charles wailed loudly as his mother finished her speech.

In November 1897, a second son, Herman, was born. In spite of Wells-Barnett's vigor and commitment to her cause, she had to face reality. She could not be an editor, activist, and mother and do justice to all three roles. She now had two sons under the age of two, and she was exhausted. She resigned as editor of *The Chicago*

Ida B. Wells-Barnett's first child was a son named Charles.

Conservator and made no more plans for speeches. She concentrated on her private life. She believed the most important thing right then was bonding with her children.

Ida Wells-Barnett did not remain long as a stay-at-home mother. A new outrage shocked her into returning to the battle against lynching. In the spring of 1899, a white mob attacked Frazier B. Baker, black postmaster of Lake City, South Carolina, in his home. Few federal jobs were still available to black people, and there was widespread

The sadness of Frazier B. Baker's wife and children can easily be seen in this picture taken of them shortly after he was lynched in 1899.

resentment among whites that Baker was the postmaster. The Baker home was set afire, and when members of the family tried to flee the flames, they were shot. Baker died inside the blazing house.

An enraged Ida Wells-Barnett joined a group of Illinois congressmen visiting the White House to protest the killing. To President William McKinley, Wells-Barnett said, "Nowhere in the civilized world save the United States of America do men, possessing all civil and political power, go out in bands of 50 and 5,000 to hunt down, shoot, hang or burn to death a single individual."[8]

President McKinley listened politely and promised to investigate the murder of Postmaster Baker and bring the lynchers to justice. Wells-Barnett spent five weeks in Washington with her nursing baby, Herman. Frustrated that no apparent action was underway, Wells-Barnett returned to Chicago. Eventually, eleven white men were arrested for Baker's murder, but a jury could not agree on their guilt, and they were all set free.

In April 1899, another lynching took place. A black man, Sam Hose, killed a white man in Georgia, claiming self-defense. Hose was seized by a mob and tortured before being burned alive. The picniclike atmosphere of the lynching scene and the involvement of prominent white men in the crime made it especially horrendous.

Wells-Barnett formed a committee to investigate the incident. They hired a detective to gather evidence.

The detective concluded that Hose had indeed acted in self-defense. Wells-Barnett then published a pamphlet entitled *Lynch Law in Georgia*, concluding that Hose was killed to teach all black people a lesson. No matter what a white man did to them black people who did not want to be lynched had better take it. In the eyes of the ruling white community, the black person—however wronged— had no right to resist.

Ida Wells-Barnett tried to enlist the aid of Booker T. Washington, founder of the well-respected Tuskegee Institute in Alabama, in her anti-lynching crusade. Washington, however, walked a thin and careful line in his approach to white people. Many very rich white men contributed large amounts of money to his school, helping black students get the education they needed. Washington did not want to endanger the good relations he had with white people in the North and the South. He believed so strongly in his educational work that he refused to risk it by joining the battle against the emotionally charged issue of lynching. Wells-Barnett was disappointed by his decision.

On the other hand, Ida Wells-Barnett was finding more support from W. E. B. DuBois, a young African-American leader who was demanding civil rights for black people and an end to all forms of oppression.

> Ida Wells-Barnett tried to enlist the aid of Booker T. Washington.

The United States was involved in the Spanish-American War, and Wells-Barnett, along with other black Americans, felt that black soldiers should be taking part in the war effort. President McKinley had issued a call for young American men to serve. Wells-Barnett traveled to Springfield, Illinois, to give support to the African-American 8th Regiment, which was mobilizing to join the war. Ultimately, four black regiments saw service in the Spanish-American War.

Ida Wells-Barnett continued to be disappointed in President McKinley, because in his message to Congress he failed to condemn the deaths of scores of black people in the wake of the Wilmington, North Carolina, riot. In November 1898, white politicians had attacked black officeholders, setting off the violence.

Chapter 9

Lonely Warrior

R esponding to the lack of justice for the victims of the Wilmington riot, Ida Wells-Barnett said at a meeting of the Afro-American Council, "We must educate the white people out of their 250 years of slave history."[1] She recognized that since white people had the political power, they were the ones who needed to be converted. They had to understand that discrimination and oppression hurt both the oppressor and the oppressed. Injustices also harmed the good name of the United States in the world community.

In 1900, the *Chicago Tribune* promoted the idea of racial segregation in the public schools. Segregation already was the rule in the South, but in the North children of all races went to school together. Wells-Barnett met with her white friend, Jane Addams, the founder of Hull House. Together they lobbied Chicago's public officials

Jane Addams started the social-work movement in the United States. Today, social workers help improve people's quality of life.

◆ ◆ ◆ ◆ ◆

against segregation. Chicago eventually gave up the idea of separating the races in public schools.

As the twentieth century began, the Barnetts lived in a two-story house on Rhodes Avenue in a pleasant mostly white neighborhood. Although blacks were not legally banned from housing in northern white neighborhoods, there was deep prejudice against them. The Barnetts were not welcome, and they knew it. When they returned home, doors were deliberately slammed in neighboring homes to express their displeasure. White children often harassed the Barnett boys, five-year-old Charles and three-year-old Herman. Once Wells-Barnett came out on her porch to warn the white boys to leave her sons alone.

Ida Wells-Barnett was a very protective mother. She was loving and kind, but firm and strict as well. When the children misbehaved, their mother could bring them in line with one of her stern looks. The Barnett children were expected to perform their chores, as Ida Wells-Barnett herself had done her chores as a child. She believed her own upbringing had prepared her well for the challenges she had to face. She visited the children's school often and asked the teachers how they were doing. Her parents had done the same for her.

The Barnetts faithfully attended Sunday church services and Sunday school. They spent Sunday afternoon reading the Bible at the dining room table. In 1901, the Barnetts welcomed a daughter, Ida, and in 1904, another daughter, Alfreda, was born. Alfreda was the Barnetts' last child.

Ida Wells-Barnett turned her attention to a new project, a black theater. The Pekin Theatre at the corner of Twenty-seventh and State streets was launched with her support and fundraising activities. Here, at last, was a theater where black patrons could sit anywhere they chose. Although inferior seating was not a matter of law in the North, it was often the custom. Black people understood they were not welcome in many places, and they were expected to move to the rear in many public places. Most, wanting to avoid a scene, did just that or stayed home. Wells-Barnett was especially pleased that the Pekin Theatre provided a training ground for black actors. She recalled her own experience giving dramatic readings in

Ida B. Wells-Barnett (center) poses with her four children. Clockwise from the right are Herman, Ida, Alfreda, and Charles.

Memphis, and how helpful it had been in the career she had chosen.

Wells-Barnett had been active in her church since she was a small child, and Bible reading had always been an important part of her life, so when she joined the Grace Presbyterian Church in Chicago and was asked to teach a men's Bible class, she eagerly accepted. She soon found that it was one of the most rewarding things she had ever done. Wells-Barnett taught twenty-five to thirty young black men each Sunday. She applied Bible truths in a commonsense way so the men could see how the lessons related to them and helped solve problems in their lives.

Then, once more, racial violence erupted in an American city, drawing Wells-Barnett's attention. This time it happened in Springfield, Illinois, in 1908. Two black men were accused of serious crimes, and a white mob organized to lynch them before they could go to trial. When law enforcement officers protected the prisoners, the white mob vented their rage against random black people in Springfield. The August 1908 riot was one of the most violent in the United States. Before order could be restored, two black men had been lynched, and more than seventy people had been injured. There was widespread property damage in the black neighborhoods.[2]

Ida Wells-Barnett brought up the subject of the Springfield riots in her men's Bible study class. The young men decided they personally had to do something about

The Men Who Would Have Been Lynched

Two black men, Joe James and George Richardson, were saved from a mob that wanted to lynch them. Joe James was charged with the murder of a white man. He was later legally tried and convicted of murder. Before Richardson could go on trial for rape, the woman who had accused him came forward and admitted she had made up the story and no rape had been committed. Richardson was set free. There is no way to know how many men who were lynched were innocent of any crime. Under the U.S. Constitution, all people deserve the right to a fair trial. Because law enforcement did their job in the case of both of these men and rescued them from a lynch mob, justice was served.

the social issues that led to crime and race riots. From this discussion emerged the Negro Fellowship League. Wells-Barnett built the league on principles from her Bible class. She told the young men that they had a Christian duty to advance social justice and help build social services for their community.[3]

The Negro Fellowship League met regularly in the Barnett home to discuss problems in the community. One of the first glaring problems Wells-Barnett saw was the total lack of recreational facilities for young black men in

Chicago. Young white men could go to the YMCA (Young Men's Christian Association) for sports, fellowship, and recreation. When a black youth appeared there, he was quickly shown the door. The only places young black men could go for relaxation were saloons, pool halls, and gambling houses, all breeding grounds for crime.

Ida Wells-Barnett went searching for an appropriate building for a black social club for men. She found an empty building at 2830 State Street and began raising money for the project. The Negro Fellowship Reading Room and Social Center was eventually opened, offering newspapers, books, games, and a piano on the first floor. Upstairs was a dormitory where a young man new in town could sleep for fifteen cents a night. Many young blacks were migrating to Chicago and other northern cities from the South, and this hotel provided a much-needed service. For three years, a white couple, allies of Wells-Barnett, paid the rent and salary for a secretary for the club.

There was also an employment office in the club building, especially useful to newcomers to the city. Ida Wells-Barnett worked there every day. Most of the regulars were men, but sometimes a young woman came for help. Wells-Barnett counseled all the young people on how to fit in with their new surroundings. Those who arrived from the South often carried with them customs that limited their chances for success. For instance, young women would wear their boudoir caps on the street.

Wells-Barnett urged them to drop this practice because it made them look like country girls without skills a city could use.

One day a frightened twenty-three-year-old woman came to the door of the club. She told a harrowing tale of having escaped from the home of a white family who had held her in virtual slavery without any pay since she was a child. She had taken the opportunity to escape, but in her haste she had left behind everything she owned, including her clothing. Now she had nothing but the clothes on her back and nowhere to go. She asked Wells-Barnett for help, because she was afraid to return to the white couple who had enslaved her and face their anger.

Wells-Barnett took the woman in and then personally visited the white family. Wells-Barnett spoke politely but firmly. She reminded them that slavery had been banned in the United States for some time. She asked that the woman's possessions be given back to her. She also told them that they owed the woman wages for the time she had spent working for them. Surprisingly, the white woman handed over all the property belonging to the former servant, and she then gave Wells-Barnett seven hundred dollars for back wages. Wells-Barnett presented the young woman with her property and the money, which enabled her to start a new life in Chicago.

Wells-Barnett knew many of the young black men in the neighborhood, and she was sadly aware of how many were arrested and jailed for minor offenses. Such young men were thrown in jail with hardened criminals. All too often a slightly misguided young man caught for stealing a small item would turn into a real criminal during his time in jail. Wells-Barnett often went to court to speak on behalf of young men, sometimes getting them leniency if they were guilty, or freeing them entirely if they had been wrongly accused.

In 1909, Ida Wells-Barnett and the nation heard of yet another lynching, this time in Cairo, Illinois. The body of a white woman had been found, and the police immediately went in search of a black suspect. The found a penniless, homeless black man in the area. "Frog" James could not prove where he had been at the time the crime was committed. No evidence linked him to the murder, but he was arrested nonetheless.

A lynch mob quickly gathered outside the jail where James was being held. Sheriff Frank Davis and a deputy removed James from his prison cell and took him out into the woods, supposedly to protect him from the mob. But the mob followed. The sheriff then took James back to town on the train. The train was met by the lynch mob, which easily took James into custody. He was taken to a central location in town, hoisted up on an arch over the heads of a wildly screaming crowd,

> A lynch mob quickly gathered outside the jail where James was being held.

and drilled with five hundred bullets. Then he was beheaded. His head was mounted on a post and the rest of his body burned.[4]

When news of the lynching spread, Sheriff Davis was suspended for failing to protect his prisoner and allow him to have a fair trial. Davis appealed his suspension to the governor and asked for his job back. All of Davis's friends united to speak up for him at the office of the governor. Nobody was scheduled to oppose the reinstatement of Sheriff Davis. Ferdinand Barnett urged his wife to go to the hearing and oppose Davis's return to his job. Ida Wells-Barnett had a young child at the time and was not eager to go, but finally she decided to go because of what she believed.

When Ida Wells-Barnett entered the office of Governor Deneen, she realized she was the only black person there. Sheriff Davis was surrounded by his prominent white supporters—bankers, lawyers, doctors, newspaper editors, and clergy. Dozens of letters in praise of Davis were read to the hearing. When the pro-Davis side was finished, Governor Deneen turned to Ida Wells-Barnett for the other side.

Ida Wells-Barnett had interviewed many eyewitnesses, and she was well-prepared. She described how Sheriff Davis knew beforehand that the mob planned to lynch James. Still, he did not keep him securely locked in jail, nor did he hire extra deputies to protect him. Wells-Barnett

Mary Church Terrell was another women who advocated for African-American rights.

◆ ◆ ◆ ◆ ◆

passionately declared that if Sheriff Davis was allowed to get away with permitting a lynching to happen as he had and then was reinstated, the flood-gates would be open in Illinois for more lynch-ings. Governor Deneen made his decision the following Tuesday morning. He ruled that Sheriff Davis had failed in his duty to protect his prisoner, and so would not be rein-stated. By his decision, the governor announced that Illinois was no safe place for lynchings. Wells-Barnett had won a major victory, and no more lynchings took place in Illinois.

In 1909, Ida Wells-Barnett and Mary Church Terrell were the only two black women invited to participate in the "Committee of 40," a conference on the status of black Americans. Held in New York City, the conference helped prepare the groundwork for what would become the National Association for the Advancement of Colored People (NAACP).[5] Though Wells-Barnett helped found the NAACP, she did not think it was dedicated enough to fighting racial injustice, so she returned to work in Chicago.

Ida Wells-Barnett saw President Woodrow Wilson in 1913 and appealed to him to end racial discrimination in federal jobs.[6] Unfortunately, the opposite happened. After Wilson was inaugurated, the segregation of blacks was strictly enforced throughout the federal government. The number of black officeholders and advisers declined sharply.

In 1913, in recognition of her years of working with black youth, Ida Wells-Barnett was offered the job of adult probation officer in Chicago on the recommendation of Judge Harry Olson, chief justice of the municipal court.[7] The job paid $150.00 a month, and Wells-Barnett accepted it.

Chapter 10

Final Years, Death, and Legacy

n May 28, 1913, Ida Wells-Barnett became the first black adult probation officer in Chicago. She was fifty-one years old. Her duties included being in the courthouse between 9:00 and 12:00 each day and then spending time in the field checking on her eighty-five probationers. She often worked with her parolees all afternoon and far into the night.

Wells-Barnett's children ranged in age from nine to seventeen. She spent as much time as she could with them, and they were all doing well. Charles was a quiet, studious boy, while Herman was charming and less dependable. Ida loved to study, but Alfreda, the youngest, was an athlete who enjoyed skating and outdoor activities.

The salary Wells-Barnett earned helped with the expenses of the Fellowship Center, which continued to provide much-needed social services. It gave Wells-Barnett great consolation that no one seeking food had ever been turned away from the pantry, nor had any homeless person been denied shelter. "We took what satisfaction we could out of the fact that we had helped a human being at the hour of his greatest need," she said later.[1]

When Ida Wells-Barnett learned that a black convict at Joliet Penitentiary was apparently being railroaded for a murder he did not commit, she swung into action. "Chicken Joe" Campbell was a trustee at the prison when a fire broke out, killing the warden's wife, Mrs. Allen. Although many people had access to the warden's quarters, the finger of suspicion pointed to Joe Campbell, the only black man there. Wells-Barnett recruited James Keeley, editor of the *Record Herald*, to focus on the story. He invited Wells-Barnett to write an article pointing out that Campbell was innocent until proven guilty. The Negro Fellowship League sent a lawyer to help defend Campbell. In spite of all their efforts, Campbell was found guilty after a trial and was sentenced to hang. Believing him completely innocent, Ferdinand Barnett appealed to the Illinois Supreme Court, which commuted the sentence to life imprisonment.

Wells-Barnett then took up the case of Steve Green, a black man in a local jail who tried to kill himself rather than face being returned to Arkansas to face murder charges. Green, a tenant farmer, had saved enough money to leave, but his white employer threatened him with death if he left the farm. In the struggle that followed, the white man was killed, and Green pleaded self-defense. Wells-Barnett hired a lawyer for Green, and he was freed.

In 1916, when there was a change in political parties in Chicago, Wells-Barnett lost her job as a probation officer, but she did not slow down her efforts on behalf of the rights of black men and women. She launched a black suffrage organization—Alpha Suffrage. Suffrage meant the right to vote. At this time women could not vote in the United States. White and black women sometimes worked together to gain this right. The Nineteenth Amendment to the U.S. Constitution, ratified in 1920, gave all women the right to vote.

In 1916, Ida Wells-Barnett also became involved in an incident in Houston, Texas, involving black soldiers. The all-black 3rd Battalion, 24th Infantry, was stationed at Fort Logan outside Houston. The local police often clashed with black soldiers, and these soldiers were beaten and arrested for minor offenses. When a false rumor spread that a black corporal, Charles Biltmore, had been killed by the police, angry black soldiers marched into town, opening fire. Sixteen whites and four blacks were killed. A swift secret court-martial sentenced nineteen black soldiers to death and forty-three to life imprisonment. The first

> Angry black soldiers marched into town, opening fire.

thirteen scheduled to be executed were not told when they would die until just hours before their hanging on December 11, 1917, thus denying them a chance to appeal.[2]

Ida Wells-Barnett believed the soldiers had been denied due process, and she held a memorial in their honor, passing out buttons condemning lynching. A white reporter for the *Herald Examiner* took one of the buttons and notified the U.S. Secret Service. The Secret Service men told Wells-Barnett that if she continued to pass out those buttons, she would be arrested for treason. They demanded that she hand over all of her buttons, but she refused. Wells-Barnett firmly told the Secret Service agents that she believed those executed soldiers had been denied their rights as American citizens, and she had the right to protest. She continued distributing her buttons until they were all gone. She was not arrested.

Ida Wells-Barnett spearheaded a program to give Christmas gifts to black soldiers. White soldiers received such gifts from white service organizations, but black soldiers had been neglected. Wells-Barnett worked with the City Federation of Colored Women's clubs to give a half-pound box of candy and other gifts to twelve hundred black soldiers.

In 1918, the Barnetts moved to an eight-room home on Chicago's Grand Avenue. Blacks were not welcome there, and several homes of black residents had been bombed. Wells-Barnett demanded action from the city officials to find and prosecute the culprits. No action was taken, and three weeks later racial tensions exploded into a full-scale riot. Armed mobs roamed Chicago, killing and burning. The Barnetts remained in their home until the violence ended.

In 1919, Ida Wells-Barnett traveled to Arkansas to fight on behalf of hundreds of men and woman who were sharecroppers trying to organize a union. Sharecroppers were tenant farmers who tilled the soil for the owner of the land in return for a share of the produce. The Arkansas black sharecroppers believed they were not being treated fairly, so they wanted to start a union that would work for their rights.

Angry white landowners accused the black sharecroppers of plotting a revolution and intending to kill white people. Twelve black sharecroppers were arrested and charged with plotting murder. In a trial that lasted less than one hour, the twelve were convicted and sentenced to death. Wells-Barnett held protest meetings and fund-raisers for the condemned men. The case dragged on for three years. Three times gallows were built and the men were scheduled to die, but last-minute appeals saved them. Wells-Barnett wrote a pamphlet entitled *The Arkansas Race Riot*, informing the whole country of the injustice in

Chicago Riot

On a Sunday afternoon in July 1919, some black boys were swimming in a part of Lake Michigan that was considered to be reserved for whites. While the beaches were not segregated by law as they were in the South, there was an understanding that each race would keep to its own area. Eugene Williams, a seventeen-year-old black boy, entered the water at the place intended for blacks, but then he drifted south into the white area.

At the same time, some other black youths walked through the white area, and a fight broke out between them and white bathers. Stones and insults flew back and forth. Frightened, Williams remained in the water, clinging to a railroad tie. When a white boy approached, Williams let go of the railroad tie and drowned. When news of what had happened spread, a riot tore through Chicago, resulting in the deaths of thirty-eight people, more than five hundred injuries, and great property destruction.[3]

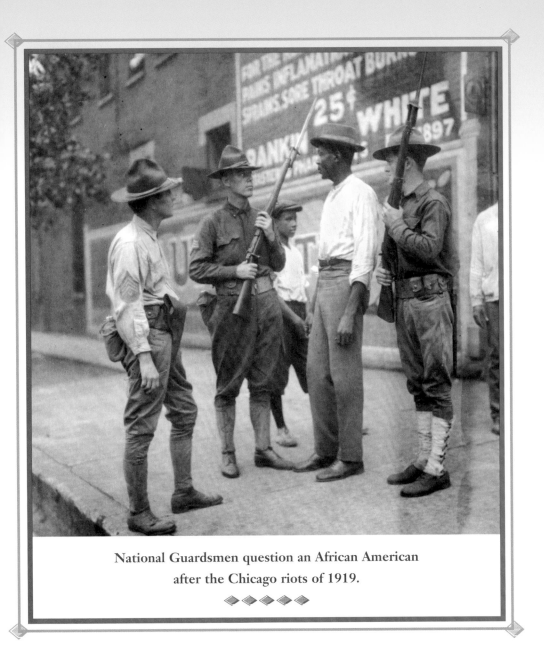

National Guardsmen question an African American
after the Chicago riots of 1919.

These are believed to be the twelve condemned men
whose lives Ida B. Wells helped save.

Arkansas. In 1923, the U.S. Supreme Court agreed with
Wells-Barnett, and all the men were set free.

Now in her sixties, Wells-Barnett was a grandmother.
Three of her children were married, and only Ida
remained at home. Wells-Barnett began to write her autobiography. She also lobbied for the Dyer Bill, which would
have imposed heavy penalties on countries where lynching
occurred, but the bill failed to pass.

The 1927 flooding of the Mississippi River caused
great destruction, and Wells-Barnett believed federal relief
efforts often ignored black victims. Frustrated by the
politicians, she ran for office herself. She campaigned for a

seat in the Illinois State Senate in 1930. But her campaign was short of funds, and she lost by a wide margin.

As the entire United States sank into economic depression in the 1930s, Wells-Barnett worked to ease suffering among the jobless and homeless blacks in Chicago.

On March 21, 1931, Ida B. Wells-Barnett came home ill after spending the day shopping. She remained in bed all day Sunday, and on Monday her husband found her incoherent. She was rushed to Dailey Hospital, where she was diagnosed with uremia, a severe kidney disease. She never regained consciousness, and she died on Wednesday, March 25, her son Charles's thirty-fifth birthday.

At Ida B. Wells-Barnett's funeral, the church was filled to overflowing. Her sons, stepsons, and nephews served as pallbearers. The service was simple and dignified. There was no widespread outpouring of public tributes because, for all the work she had done on behalf of blacks who were victims of injustice and against the horror of lynching, she did not become famous in her lifetime.

Ida B. Wells-Barnett never completed her autobiography. Her daughter gathered all her notes after her death, and it was finally published in 1970 as *Crusade for Justice: The Autobiography of Ida B. Wells.*

In 1940, a public-housing project was named for Wells-Barnett—the Ida B. Wells Garden Homes. The project covers forty-seven acres and houses seven thousand people, serving the kind of disadvantaged people

This Chicago Housing Authority poster advertises the
opening of Ida B. Wells Homes in 1940.

Wells-Barnett spent her life serving. Many schools in the United States bear Wells-Barnett's name, including the Ida B. Wells School in Jamaica, New York; the Ida B. Wells Continuation High School in San Francisco, California; the Ida B. Wells Community Academy School District in Akron, Ohio; and the Ida B. Wells Academy in Milwaukee, Wisconsin.

A public broadcasting special in 1989, "Ida B. Wells: A Passion for Justice," brought her story to the attention of millions unfamiliar with her work. In a moment of despair after she could no longer keep the Negro Fellowship Reading Room open, Wells-Barnett expressed in her auto-biography regret that she had not accomplished much. "I had nothing to show for all those years of toil and labor," she lamented.[4] Yet she had touched the lives of so many in trouble, and her passionate and relentless crusade against lynching had turned the tide of public opinion against the crime. She had prepared the ground for the movement that would wipe lynching from the face of America.[5]

Probably one of the tributes that she would most appreciate is the Ida B. Wells-Barnett University Professorship that was established at DePaul University in 1999. The professorship was set up to achieve the ideal for which Well-Barnett had struggled—a more just, humane society. In 2003, Chicago journalist Laura S. Washington joined DePaul University as the Ida B. Wells-Barnett pro-fessor. Two of Wells-Barnett's grandsons, Benjamin C.

Dan Duster (right), great grandson of Ida B. Wells-Barnett, speaks with Joseph Jordan, curator of an exhibit of lynching photographs on display at the Martin Luther King, Jr., historic site visitors' center in Atlanta on January 8, 2003.

Duster and Donald L. Duster, carried on the tradition of education that their grandmother had cherished, by graduating from DePaul University.

In June 2005, Democratic Senator Mary Landrieu of Louisiana, and Republican Senator George Allen from Virginia paid tribute to the work of Ida Wells-Barnett from the floor of the U.S. Senate. Calling lynching "an American form of terrorism," they praised Wells-Barnett for her fearless crusade against it. The U.S. Senate passed a resolution apologizing for never having passed anti-lynching legislation.[6]

Landrieu recounted the long struggle that Wells-Barnett had waged against lynching after the murder of her friends at The People's Grocery. "She wrote and she spoke and she tried to gather pictures to tell a story to a nation that simply refused to believe," Landrieu said.[7]

Continuing the process of giving belated recognition to Ida Wells-Barnett, the Ida B. Wells Museum in Holly Springs, Mississippi, has been renovated, reopening to the public in 2005. Three hundred commemorative bricks were sold for $150.00 each to help defray the expenses. The city of Holly Springs now proudly calls attention to the woman many hailed in her lifetime as the "Princess of the Press." She is cited in the museum as a native daughter of Holly Springs who fought tirelessly for justice and equality.

Chronology

1862—Ida Bell Wells born July 16 in Holly Springs, Mississippi.

1865—Wells family and all slaves freed after Civil War.

1878—Loses both parents and brother in yellow fever epidemic; becomes elementary school teacher.

1883—Moves to Memphis, Tennessee, to teach there.

1884—Expelled from seat on Chesapeake and Ohio Railroad for refusing to move to the railroad car for black passengers.

1886—Begins writing articles for local newspapers.

1889—Becomes part owner of the newspaper *Memphis Free Speech*.

1892—Begins anti-lynching crusade when friend is lynched in Memphis.

1893—Publishes anti-lynching pamphlet, *Southern Horrors: Lynch Law in all its Phases*.

1895—Marries Ferdinand L. Barnett. Publishes pamphlet *A Red Record. Tabulated Statistics and Alleged Causes of Lynchings in the United States*.

1896—Son Charles born March 25.

1897—Son Herman born November 18.

1901—Daughter Ida born.

1904—Daughter Alfreda born.

IDA B. WELLS-BARNETT

1909—Helps found National Association for the Advancement of Colored People (NAACP).

1910—Founds Negro Fellowship League.

1913—Becomes adult probation officer in Chicago; founds first club for African-American women to advocate for voting rights for women.

1923—U.S. Supreme Court cancels the death sentences of twelve black sharecroppers after Ida B. Wells-Barnett campaigned to save them from execution.

1930—Runs unsuccessfully for a seat in Illinois State Senate.

1931—Dies in Chicago on March 25.

Chapter Notes

Chapter 1. The First Battle

1. Peter Carr Black, "A Courageous Voice for Civil Rights," *Mississippi History Now: Mississippi Historical Society*, © 2000–2004 <http://mshistory.k12.ms.us/features/feature13/ida_wells.html> (June 1, 2007).

2. Lee D. Baker, "Ida B. Wells-Barnett and Her Passion for Justice," April 1996, <http://www.duke.edu/~IDbaker/classes/AAIH/caaih/ibwells/ibwbkgrd.html> (June 1, 2007).

3. Ibid.

4. Alfreda M. Duster, ed., *Crusade for Justice: The Autobiography of Ida B. Wells* (Chicago: The University of Chicago Press, 1970), p. 19.

5. Linda McMurry, *To Keep the Waters Troubled: The Life of Ida B. Wells* (New York: Oxford University Press, 1998), p. 29.

Chapter 2. Mississippi Childhood

1. Alfreda M. Duster, ed., *Crusade for Justice: The Autobiography of Ida B. Wells* (Chicago: The University of Chicago Press, 1970), p. 10.

2. Ibid.

3. Patti Carr Black, "Ida B. Wells: A Courageous Voice for Civil Rights," *Mississippi History* Now:

Mississippi Historical Society, © 2000–2004 <http://mhistory.k12.ms.us/features/feature13/ida_wells.html> (June 1, 2007).

    4. John Hope Franklin and August Meier, eds., *Black Leaders of the 20th Century* (Chicago: University of Illinois Press, 1983), p. 40.

    5. Black, p. 1.

Chapter 3. Head of the Family and Teacher

    1. Bob Arnebeck, "A Short History of Yellow Fever," n.d., <http://www.geocities.com/bobarnebeck/history.html> (June 1, 2007).

    2. Ibid.

    3. Dorothy Sterling, *Black Foremothers: Three Lives* (New York: Feminist Press, 1988), p. 66.

    4. Alfreda M. Duster, ed., *Crusade for Justice: The Autobiography of Ida B. Wells* (Chicago: The University of Chicago Press, 1970), p. 12.

    5. Ibid., p. 16.

    6. Ibid., p. 22.

    7. "Ida B. Wells," *Tennessee History Preservation and Educational Artifacts*, n.d., <http://www.vic.com/tnchron/class/Ida.html> (December 2006).

Chapter 4. The Birth of a Journalist

    1. John Hope Franklin and August Meier, eds., *Black Leaders of the 20th Century* (Chicago: University of Illinois Press, 1983), p. 41.

CHAPTER NOTES

2. "Ida B. Wells," *Tennessee History Preservation and Educational Artifacts*, n.d., <http://www.vic.com/tnchron/class/Ida.html> (December 2006).

3. Linda McMurry, *To Keep the Waters Troubled: The Life of Ida B. Wells* (New York: Oxford University Press, 1998), p. 78.

4. Alfreda M. Duster, ed., *Crusade for Justice: The Autobiography of Ida B. Wells* (Chicago: The University of Chicago Press, 1970), p. 23.

5. Ibid.

6. Ibid., p. 24.

7. McMurry, p. 42.

8. Dorothy Sterling, *Black Foremothers: Three Lives* (New York: Feminist Press, 1988) p. 69.

9. Duster, p. 24.

10. Sterling, p. 69.

11. McMurry, p. 79.

12. Ibid.

13. Duster, p. 31.

Chapter 5. "The Brilliant Iola"

1. Alfreda M. Duster, ed., *Crusade for Justice: The Autobiography of Ida B. Wells* (Chicago: The University of Chicago Press, 1970), p. 31.

2. "Ida Wells Barnett," Tennessee State Library, n.d., <http://www.tnstate.edu/library/digital/wells.htm> (May 7, 2007).

3. Dorothy Sterling, *Black Foremothers: Three Lives* (New York: Feminist Press, 1988), pp. 75–76.

4. Patti Carr Black, "Ida B. Wells: A Courageous Voice for Civil Rights," *Mississippi History Now: Mississippi Historical Society*, © 2000–2004, <http://mshistory.k12. ms.us/features/feature13/ida_wells.html> (June 1, 2007), p. 3.

5. Duster, p. 37.

6. "The Booker T. Washington Papers," University of Illinois Press, n.d., <http://www.historycooperative. org/btw/Vol.2/html/index.html> (June 1, 2007), p. 357.

Chapter 6. Outrage in Memphis

1. Alfreda M. Duster, ed., *Crusade for Justice: The Autobiography of Ida B. Wells* (Chicago: The University of Chicago Press, 1970), p. 47.

2. Ibid., p. 57.

3. "Senate Apologizes for Not Enacting Anti-Lynching Legislation," *Democracy Now*, June 14, 2005, <http://democracynow.org/article.pl?sid=05/06/14/ 1350253> (May 7, 2007).

4. "Ida B. Wells-Barnett," *The Tennessee Encyclopedia of History and Culture*, October 24, 2005, <http:// tennesseeencyclopdeia.net/imagegallery/php?EntryID= w041> (May 7, 2007).

5. "Senate Apologizes for Not Enacting Anti-Lynching Legislation."

6. "Ida B. Wells," *Tennessee History Preservation and Educational Artifacts*, n.d., <http://www.vic.com/tnchron/ class/Ida.html> (January 2007).

7. "Ida B. Wells-Barnett," *Black History*, n.d., <http://www.gale.com/free_resources/bhm/bio/wells_i. htm> (June 1, 2007).

8. John Hope Franklin and August Meier, eds., *Black Leaders of the 20th Century* (Chicago: University of Chicago Press, 1983), p. 41.

9. "Ida B. Wells-Barnett," *Black History*.

10. Ibid.

11. Franklin and Meier, p. 42.

Chapter 7. No Peace, No Justice

1. John Hope Franklin and August Meier, eds., *Black Leaders of the 20th Century* (Chicago: University of Illinois Press, 1980), p. 43.

2. Ibid.

3. Patricia A. Schechter, "Ida B. Wells-Barnett and American Reform, 1880-1930," Fall 2001, <http:// uncpress.unc.edu/chapters/schechter_ida.html> (May 7, 2007).

4. Alfreda M. Duster, ed., *Crusade for Justice: The Autobiography of Ida B. Wells* (Chicago: The University of Chicago Press, 1970), p. 98.

5. Ibid., p. 117.

Chapter 8. "Brave Woman!"

1. Lee D. Baker, "Ida B. Wells-Barnett and Her Passion for Justice," April 1996, <http://www.duke.edu/ ~Idbaker/classes/AAIH/caaih/ibwells/ibwbkgrd.html> (June 1, 2007).

2. Ida Wells-Barnett, *The Red Record. The Project Gutenberg eBook*, February 8, 2005, <http://www.gutenberg.org/files/14977/14977-8.txt> (May 7, 2007), Preface.

3. Ibid., Chapter 3.

4. Ibid., Chapter 5.

5. Ibid.

6. Linda McMurry, *To Keep the Waters Troubled: The Life of Ida B. Wells* (New York: Oxford University Press, 1998), p. 238.

7. Alfreda M. Duster, ed., *Crusade for Justice: The Autobiography of Ida B. Wells* (Chicago: The University of Chicago Press, 1970), pp. 243, 251.

8. "Killing the Messenger: Ida Wells-Barnett Protests a Postmaster's Murder in 1898," *History Matters*, n.d., <http://historymatters.gmu.edu/d/56> (May 7, 2007), p. 1.

Chapter 9. Lonely Warrior

1. John Hope Franklin and August Meier, eds., *Black Leaders of the 20th Century* (Chicago: University of Illinois Press, 1983), p. 46.

2. Rayford W. Logan and Irving S. Cohen, *The American Negro* (Boston: Houghton Mifflin Company, 1967), p. 157.

3. Patricia A. Schechter, "Ida B. Wells-Barnett and American Reform, 1880–1930," n.d., <http://uncpress.unc.du/chapters/schechter_ida.htm> (June 1, 2007).

CHAPTER NOTES

4. Alfreda M. Duster, ed., *Crusade for Justice: The Autobiography of Ida B. Wells* (Chicago: The University of Chicago Press, 1970), pp. 309–310.

5. "Ida B. Wells," *Tennessee History Classroom*, n.d., http://www.tennesseehistory.com/class/Ida.htm> (May 7, 2007), p. 6.

6. "Ida B. Wells-Barnett," *Black History*, n.d., <http://www.gale.com/free_resources/bhm/bio/wells_i.htm> (June 1, 2007).

7. Ibid.

Chapter 10. Final Years, Death, and Legacy

1. Alfreda M. Duster, ed., *Crusade for Justice: The Autobiography of Ida B. Wells* (Chicago: The University of Chicago Press, 1970), p. 333.

2. "The Rise and Fall of Jim Crow," *Jim Crow Stories*, 2002, <http://www.pbs.org/wnet/jimcrow/stories-_events_ww1.html> (May 7, 2007), p. 1.

3. Richard Wade, ed., *The Negro in American Life* (New York: Houghton Mifflin, 1970), p. 141.

4. Duster, p. 414.

5. Patricia A. Schechter, "Ida B. Wells-Barnett and American Reform, 1880–1930, n.d., <http://uncpress.unc.edu/chapters/schechter_ida.html> (June 1, 2007).

6. "Senate Apologizes for Not Enacting Anti-Lynching Legislation," *Democracy Now*, June 14, 2005, <http://www.democracy.now.org/articles.pl?sid-05/06/14/1350253> (May 7, 2007).

7. Ibid., p.3.

Further Reading

BIOGRAPHIES OF IDA B. WELLS-BARNETT

Fradin, Dennis Brindell, et al. *Ida B. Wells: Mother of the Civil Rights Movement*. New York: Clarion Books, 2000.

Moore, Heidi. *Ida B. Wells-Barnett*. Chicago: Heinemann Library, 2004.

Welch, Catherine. *Ida B. Wells-Barnett—Powerhouse With a Pen*. Minneapolis: Carolrhoda Books, 2000.

COLLECTIVE BIOGRAPHIES OF IDA B. WELLS-BARNETT AND OTHER WOMEN

Coddon, Karin S. *Black Women Activists*. San Diego: Greenhaven Press, 2004.

Fullen, Marilyn K. *Great Black Writers: Biographies*. Greensboro, N.C.: Open Hand Publishing, 2002.

Gourley, Catherine. *Society's Sisters: Stories of Women Who Fought for Social Justice in America*. Bookfield, Conn.: Twenty-First Century Books, 2003.

Harness, Cheryl. *Rabble Rousers: 20 Women Who Made a Difference*. New York: Dutton Children's Books, 2003.

Pinkney, Andrea Davis. *Let It Shine: Stories of Black Women Freedom Fighters*. San Diego: Harcourt, 2000.

Rau, Dana Meachen. *Great Women of the Suffrage Movement*. Minneapolis: Compass Point Books, 2006.

CHAPTER NOTES

BOOKS ON OTHERS WHO FOUGHT FOR CIVIL RIGHTS

Altman, Susan. *Extraordinary African-Americans*. New York: Children's Press, 2001.

Fradin, Dennis Brindell, and Judith Bloom Fradin. *Fight On!: Mary Church Terrell's Battle for Integration*. New York: Clarion Books, 2003.

Karson, Jill, ed. *The Civil Rights Movement*. Farmington Hills, Mich.: Greenhaven Press, 2005.

———. *Leaders of the Civil Rights Movement*. Farmington Hills, Mich.: Greenhaven Press, 2005.

Russell, Sharman Apt. *Frederick Douglass: Abolitionist Editor*. Philadelphia: Chelsea House, 2005.

Internet Addresses

Ida B. Wells-Barnett Biography
Very colorful and exciting with good photographs
<www.africawithin.com.bios/ida-wells.htm>

Ida B. Wells-Barnett. What You Need to Know About African American History
Good overview of the period in which Wells worked
<afroamhistory.about.com>

"Jim Crow Stories: Ida B. Wells." From "The Rise and Fall of Jim Crow," from PBS
Excellent photos, documents, and original sources
<www.pbs.org/wnet/jimcrow/>

Index